# *Healing the Nations*

## Fred Kaan

**The Man and his Hymns**

*to Anne:*

*with love!*

*Fred.*

D1638049

*Gillian R. Warson*

First published in 2006 by
Stainer & Bell Ltd, 23 Gruneisen Road, London N3 1DZ, England

**Also available:**
*The Only Earth We Know*, a collection of hymn texts by Fred Kaan
(Stainer & Bell/Hope Publishing Company USA, 1999).

**British Library Cataloguing-in-Publication Data**
A catalogue record of this book is available from the British Library

ISBN 0 85249 889 6 / 978 0 85249 889 7

The cover design shows the lectern falls designed by Fred Kaan for
Pilgrim Church, Plymouth (see pages 61–62). Photographs by the author.

Printed in Great Britain by Caligraving Ltd, Thetford, Norfolk

# Contents

*This book is dedicated to the childhood penfriend who
introduced Fred to England and English ways,
Dear Brother Scout – Peter Hayward (1928–2006).*

I would like to thank Fred and Anthea, for their wonderful hospitality and conversation, John, Dennis and Richard, for reading the manuscript, and the following people who have made this project so interesting and enjoyable:

*Holland*
Dr Albert van den Heuvel from the World Council of Churches
Hanneke Kortman & Aagje from the Moravian Settlement in Zeist
Greet and Look Plekker from the Hannie Schaft Foundation
Mr and Mrs Salamink from Louise de Colignyplein 15

*Windsor Road URC, Barry*
Marian and Hector Downes, Janice and Colin Proctor,
Christine Roberts

*Pilgrim Church, Plymouth*
Doug and May Barkell, Kath Hancock, Val Harris,
Christine Reid, Mrs Joyce Warren

*General Secretary of URC (1992–2001)*
Tony Burnham

*Central Church, Swindon*
Mrs Caroline Cairns, Mrs Nancy Dale

*Penhill URC*
Mr Albert Roberts

I would also like to thank The Pratt Green Trust for their generous financial support towards my travel expenses for researching this book.

# 1

## Glenridding 2005

I am in the front seat of the bright red Fiesta – Anthea, Fred Kaan's second wife, having kindly scrambled into the back. As we hurtle along the winding roads they continue their earlier conversation, allowing me a few minutes to collect my thoughts. Their talk is of rail and bus tickets lost and found. A few days after my departure Fred and Anthea will be leaving for Canada to take part in a hectic round of lecturing and hymn-singing. There has been some confusion over the travelling arrangements and the tickets sent do not quite match those requested. And the ones sent have been mislaid anyway! In order to conduct this conversation, Fred apparently needs to keep turning his head to address Anthea, which causes me some concern as straight ahead there lies the steely-grey expanse of Ullswater. I need not have worried as Fred comes to a controlled halt. 'You have to be careful here,' he twinkles. 'Some of our friends have gone straight over!' The journey continues along the lakeshore. The scenery is breathtakingly beautiful, even on this sunless day at the very beginning of January. Trees bend over the water, and beyond, the heather-covered mountains rise in Wordsworthian grandeur. Somehow, it seems the perfect setting for the contemporary lyricist beside me, Fred Kaan, who has been writing hymns for over forty years. The scenery is all that Wordsworth and Fred Kaan share. Fred is a self-confessed enemy of hillwalking and indeed as a Dutchman shuns slopes of any kind! He says, 'I allow other people to enjoy the physical exercise while I stay at home to check that the red wine is chambré.' Fred turns to Anthea and invites her to tell me the story of how the Lake District came to be their home.

Anthea's parents had visited the Lake District each year for walking holidays. Year after year they stayed at the same guest house, but always without making reservations. One summer, they arrived to find there were no vacancies. They were recommended to continue along the road until they reached the next village, Glenridding. This they did and happened upon some building plots. Uncharacteristically, they did not hesitate to snap up the opportunity to purchase a plot. On this site a cosy bungalow was built where they enjoyed many happy holidays. Later, they spent a happy retirement there, and the house became a place of refuge for Anthea and her own family. Eventually, after her husband died, Anthea's mother became too frail to live there on her own and moved to Kendal. After Fred and Anthea married, Anthea suggested that they should also spend their retirement in the house where she recalled so many happy memories. Anthea was anxious about Fred's reaction to this suggestion, as he had spent the greater part of his life in cities. However, he was sure he could enjoy the mountains without climbing them! Both declare that their move to the Lake District was the best thing they ever did.

Our car journey continued for about forty minutes and finally we wove our way up the steep lane to *Marazan*. I was shown to my charming bedroom with a view looking on to the steep slope of the garden. I had a few minutes to myself to think about how I had come to be working with Fred Kaan, who had always been something of an idol for me!

When I was a little girl I loved singing – especially singing hymns. Sitting on the school hall floor, I was perfectly content to chortle out platitudes about silver daisies, golden buttercups and purple-headed mountains. However, we didn't see too many of the latter in Stevenage New Town. I was all the more delighted when we were presented with a brand new hymn book with a smart red-white-and-blue cover. This was, of course, *100 Hymns for Today*. Now I had the opportunity to sing about some of the things I saw every day such as 'crowded streets and council flats'. It was not for some years that I realised that many of these texts, often sung to familiar tunes, were all by the same person. A writer with a striking name – cosy, familiar Fred followed by exotic Kaan with its alluring double 'a' in the middle.

Thirty years later, in 2000, I attended the annual conference of The Hymn Society of Great Britain and Ireland. I was absolutely delighted to be introduced to the distinguished Dutchman with his shock of silver hair and crinkles round his eyes. We spent several hours chatting and Fred Kaan made me a present of his most recent collection *The Only Earth We Know*, which had been published to coincide with his seventieth birthday. We talked about his hymns and hymn writing in general, especially the current 'hot potato' of 'multi-faith hymnody' – a subject on which we were in total agreement! I was drawn to Fred's commitment to the environment, to unity and to peace. I wanted to know more about him and – fortunately – he was happy to share his life-story with me.

# 2

## Haarlem 1929–1939

Frederik Herman Kaan, the elder son of Hermanus Kaan and Brandina Kaan Prinsen, was born on 27 July 1929 in the pretty Dutch city of Haarlem, on the Spaarne River. Haarlem is the capital of Noord Holland and twenty miles from Amsterdam. It is a city of cultural and historical importance and has been a busy centre for trade in hyacinth and tulip bulbs. The residents of Haarlem have a reputation for being culturally astute and somewhat aloof, partly because the city was the home of Laurens Janszoon Coster, to whom the Dutch ascribe the invention of the printing press.

Dutch children, even when they grow up, tend to prefer living in their old neighbourhood near their families. Brandina and Hermanus chose to make their first married home in Haarlem because Hermanus's mother, Gerredina van Huizen, lived there. Her husband, Frederik, after whom Fred was named, was a local tradesman and sold paraffin from a barrow in the street. Hermanus and Brandina lived for the first few years of their married life in a typically Dutch terraced house on Voorhelmstraat. They were not a religious family, but Fred was baptised in the spectacular Saint Bavo Cathedral, also called the *Groote Kerk*. This vast edifice, built in the fifteenth century and recorded in the paintings of the 17th-century Dutch master Pieter Saenredam (1597–1665), houses one of the biggest organs in the world, with over five thousand pipes. The cathedral's importance at the hub of the city was assured as many tiny shops and businesses were built into its massive walls and can be seen there to this day. In spite of this impressive introduction to the Christian life, Fred did not set foot inside a church again until his mid-teens!

Brandina's family came from Zeist, a much smaller town near one of Holland's most prominent university cities, Utrecht. Brandina's father was a baker and was relatively wealthy since he was the only baker in Zeist. His name, somewhat confusingly, was also Hermanus and he gave his name to Fred's younger brother, who was born in 1932. Although not overtly religious, Grandfather Herman was a right-wing Christian with a strong sense of the importance of tradition. Each day, dressed in black and like an Old Testament patriarch, he would declaim passages from the Bible in traditional pronunciation. He had strong political convictions and was a passionate supporter of the Boers in the Boer War (1899–1902). This resulted in his travelling to Brussels with guns secreted in his luggage, and even sailing as far as South Africa to supply the Boers with arms.

Neither of Fred's parents was formally educated beyond primary school. Hermanus, though, had a job as an office worker for the Nederlandse Spoorwegen (Netherlands Railways). He was enthusiastic and anxious to improve himself.

He worked his way through the ranks to the position of draughtsman and ultimately became an accident inspector. This meant that in 1934 the family moved to Amersfoort, near Utrecht, an important junction where the technical section of the Dutch railways was situated.

Brandina had attended a domestic science college in her home town of Zeist. After her marriage to Hermanus, she devoted herself to her family. Brandina was anxious to see her parents and brothers regularly. She found that she could not settle either in Haarlem or Amersfoort and, after a few years, managed to persuade Hermanus to move to Zeist where her parents and brothers still lived and then the family were able to enjoy frequent visits. Now Hermanus had a longer journey to work, which he had to make on a motorcycle. In the evenings the little boys would go out to meet him and ride the remainder of the journey home sitting on the fuel tank.

Zeist is an interesting town both architecturally and historically. During the eighteenth century Count Nikolaus Ludwig von Zinzendorf purchased the manor house with the vision of forming a settlement for the Moravian Church, which was at that time subject to savage persecution. His idea was not only to have a 'beautiful house and an exquisite garden, but a city of God'. For many years the Moravian settlement was the hub of the community in Zeist. Two separate quadrangles were built, one for women and one for men. These were called the *Zusterplein* and *Broederplein*. Members of the community had shops and businesses which were incorporated into the design and these were patronised by people from the town. Although, when they first moved to Zeist, the Kaan family had little interest in religious matters, Brandina had many German-speaking female friends in the Moravian community and learned to speak excellent German herself. She was musical and, playing the piano, accompanied herself singing German Lieder, and taught her young sons German folk songs.

The Kaans's house in Zeist was newly built and situated in a leafy area of the town. All the streets in the neighbourhood were named after prominent Dutch women – mostly wives of counts and princes. Louise de Colignyplein 15 was in the middle of a terrace, and immediately opposite was a small wooded area, giving the street a rural, secluded feel. The three-storeyed house had a small front garden and, behind the back yard, a passage led away to join a warren of other passages and entrances. The Kaans lived in this house for ten years and during this time it was to be the centre of much activity.

Hermanus and Brandina had strong political views and these were evident in the Kaan household. The Netherlands was experiencing an economic crisis by the time Fred was born. Throughout the 1920s, while the rest of Europe was sliding towards economic depression, the Netherlands had been cushioned from its worst effects by its rich holdings in the Dutch East Indies (present-day Indonesia). However, because its economy was very closely connected with that of Germany, the Depression eventually hit the Netherlands as badly as any other country in Western Europe, and the Dutch people felt the approach of their government was insufficiently radical to solve the crisis. Some felt a socialist solution was needed and others felt that fascism would provide an answer. Hermanus was passionate in his political views and was a member of the left-wing organisation the *Sociaal-Democratische Partij*. He was proud of the fact he was known as the Red Rebel – '*de rooie rakker*'. His beliefs always tended towards extremes and he sternly disapproved of drinking alcohol, which led him to form the Railway Men's Abstinence Society. Brandina shared her husband's left-wing opinions and rejected her father's right-wing views. Nevertheless, she inherited the uncompromising passion her father brought to his convictions. This was evident in her later wartime activities.

Brought up in this politically aware environment, Fred himself learned the need for a strong social conscience – a characteristic which became evident in his ministry and hymns.

# 3

## Zeist 1939-1945

Fred abruptly woke up to the harsh reality of politics when, in early May 1940, the Germans invaded Holland. Although the Dutch people had anxieties immediately preceding the invasion, they had been given assurances from Hitler himself that the Dutch neutrality enjoyed in the First World War would be respected again should a second European war break out. It was therefore a shock to everyone when on 10 May the Germans suddenly bombed the city of Rotterdam, causing an appalling loss of life and property. Although the Dutch fought bravely for five days, the superiority of the German war machine was evident. On 15 May, they surrendered and Holland was under German rule.

From the very earliest days of the Occupation, it was impressed upon the eleven-year-old Fred and his eight-year-old brother that in no circumstances were they to discuss any details of their home life with anyone outside the immediate family. The reason for this was that the Kaan family quickly became involved in the Resistance movement with Hermanus taking a leading role. Zeist itself was not in the front line of resistance activities because, unlike Amsterdam and Rotterdam, it had no large factories or rail terminals. This meant that the group in Zeist was not involved in the high-profile acts associated with resistance bravery such as blowing up factories and railway lines. Zeist was, however, of strategic importance for the collection and caching of arms. In this cause, Brandina demonstrated that she was her father's daughter, and with the help of Hermanus, Fred and Herman, dug underneath the kitchen and lounge of the house to provide a hiding place for small arms. Luckily, excavation was not difficult as the land on which the house was built was sandy. One important function of the Zeist cell was to hide and distribute arms which were dropped by the Allied Forces. This was a dangerous undertaking but it was not without its unexpected benefits. On one occasion, Brandina was able to collect some parachute silk to make into clothing – very necessary with the growing scarcities in occupied Holland. The arms were stored under the Kaans's house until required by the Resistance when their distribution was co-ordinated by Hermanus. Frequently, these arms were carried by Brandina herself who would walk the streets under the noses of the Germans with a large basket of guns concealed beneath firewood. The two young boys were trusted implicitly by their parents. On one occasion a young Resistance leader came with Hermanus to deposit some guns in the hiding place under the house. He contended that the brothers were far too young and unreliable to be part of what was going on and that they should be sent into another room. Brandina, however, was confident that the boys would never disclose anything that they had seen and insisted that the boys remain present throughout the operation. The parents' trust was not misplaced and the boys played their part throughout the Occupation without ever breathing a word to anyone.

In the early years of the war, Fred was not fully aware of the plight of the Jews. Holland had long been a place of sanctuary, and in the late 1930s and early 1940s was one of the last countries to allow Jews to settle within its borders. Jewish families and their businesses had flourished in Holland for centuries and, although the cultures did not really mix because of the social structure of Dutch society, they existed amicably alongside each other. Early in the German Occupation, life quickly became difficult for Jews living in Holland. The first anti-Jewish measures were taken in 1940 when Jewish people were forbidden to hold civic positions. In 1942 these measures culminated in Dutch Jews aged 16 to 40 being sent to do 'Labour Service' in Germany. The Dutch Jews were by character obedient people and many initially interpreted the word 'labour' simply as 'employment opportunity'. They felt that they might as well go and work in Germany as they had no jobs in Holland. During the first year of deportation some 110,000 Jews quite willingly left Holland, taking personal possessions with them. However, it was not long before the gravity of the situation became clear. Stories of what was happening in the labour camps started to leak back to Holland, and for those Jews still at liberty deportation became a threat to be avoided at all costs. For these Jews the only option was to go into hiding, or to *onderduiken* – to submerge. Everyone has heard about the plight of Anne Frank's family, but this was only one among thousands of families who took refuge in the homes of ordinary Dutch gentiles.

The Kaans had some Jewish neighbours living only a few doors from them. They were easily recognisable by the yellow star they were forced to wear. Fred used to visit them often as the man of the house was a fine musician and engineer. He devised a mechanism that allowed wind players to regulate the passage of air to their instruments during long musical phrases by using their feet. This was taken up by musicians in many of the larger orchestras in Europe. Fred realised the full implications of the situation for the Jews when one night the couple were simply taken away. Although it is well known that the entire Frank family, along with several other acquaintances, all hid in one small apartment, it was much more usual for individual Jews to go into hiding. As Resistance workers, Brandina and Hermanus felt compelled to help their Jewish compatriots. It was a big decision as there were severe penalties for being caught hiding Jews. It was not a capital offence, as in Poland, but it still carried the threat of being sent to the notorious labour camp at Mauthausen in Austria. There were also immense practical difficulties. Naturally, those in hiding lost their identities, and could obtain food and other essential supplies only on the black market, so the whole operation needed careful planning. In spite of these difficulties, one day Hermanus and Brandina called the two brothers together to reveal the secret that they had decided to take a young Jewish woman into the house to *onderduiken*.

In order to do this, it was necessary to make a number of preparations. The first and most important task was to construct a secure hiding place in the house. It turned out that this was not as difficult as they had first thought. Hermanus, along with other Resistance workers, realised that on the first floor, underneath the stairs leading to the second floor, there was a 'dead' space behind two connecting wardrobes. These had a door apiece but there was no access to a small space directly under the stairs. They made an entrance through to the area and cushioned the floor with mattresses to make it comfortable. They created a secret entrance to the newly created room that could be opened only from the inside.

As Hermanus was an officer for the local branch of the Resistance, he knew personally many of the key activists. One of these was a young woman called Hannie Schaft, who undertook many dangerous missions, which sometimes involved shooting German officers, executing collaborators and blowing up key industrial sites. She also participated in creating new identities for Jewish people, and she would steal identity cards from public places such as theatre cloakrooms and swimming-pool changing rooms. Hannie Schaft, immortalised in the film *Het Meisje met het Rode Haar*, was well known to the Gestapo and consequently was herself forced to move from place to place. On one occasion she visited the Kaans to talk about the plight of the Jews, and Fred can remember this.

Hannie had two close university friends, one called Sonja Frenk and the other Philine Polak. Both Sonja and Philine were Jewish. All three young women worked hard for the Resistance, but eventually it became too dangerous for Philine and Sonja to move about freely. They were forced to

*onderduiken* in the home of Hannie's parents in Van Dortstraat
in Haarlem. However, because their address was known to
the Germans, a safer place needed to be found. Since Hermanus already knew Hannie and her family, it was decided
that Philine should go to the Kaans's house in Louise de
Colignyplein. Although the Kaans experienced many raids
– *razzias* – carried out by the Germans, her hiding place was
never discovered. Philine lived with the family for two-and-
a-half years, joining them for meals, enjoying animated discussions and helping Fred with his Latin homework. The
Kaans were under constant threat all the time Philine lived
with them, but they never considered the personal risk that
they were taking. While Philine was living at Louise de
Colignyplein, the Nazis mounted a raid on Hannie Schaft's
house in Van Dortstraat, although Hannie had not lived there
herself for some years. Following this raid Hannie's parents
were arrested and sent to the concentration camp at Vught
where they were detained for nine months.

Philine was unable to leave the house during the day the
whole time she was living with the Kaans. Occasionally,
in the dead of night, she and Hermanus would slip out
and wander in the small copse opposite the house. Philine
found life in hiding claustrophobic, and she was desperate to
return to active Resistance work. One night she decided
that the only answer was to leave the relative safety of Louise
de Colignyplein 15 and take her chances with her former
colleagues. With only her overcoat and a small bag, she
left for the centre of Amsterdam. Fred never heard from
her again. Had she been arrested the same night? As the
Kaans speculated amongst themselves, they thought that

this was the most likely outcome. Philine had a distinctive appearance and was easily recognisable as Jewish – especially to those who were out to capture an entire race. However, it turns out that, with the help of Hannie, Philine hid in the house of a German woman, Marie Korts, where she spent the rest of the war. Afterwards Philine moved to the USA and worked for the United Nations in Washington. Sonja Frenk was arrested before the end of the war, and died in Auschwitz in November 1943. Hannie Schaft was herself captured by the Gestapo and shot in 1944.

Of course, life in Louise de Colignyplein 15 was extremely tense. The Kaans became adept at avoiding discovery. The first essential was to observe the rule of absolute secrecy. No details were ever discussed outside the house and this is probably the reason why they were left to speculate about Philine's fate as such things could be mentioned only among their closest circle. The Kaans also managed to discover a weakness in the German mentality that proved very useful. It transpired that the Germans had an abiding dread of infectious diseases such as typhoid and scarlet fever. If anyone in a house had such a disease, the authorities had to be notified, and a sign stating that an infected person was inside clearly displayed on the front door. By good fortune, Brandina's brother was a printer. He supplied the Kaans with several such signs and, when they heard that a *razzia* was to take place, they simply hung the sign on the door. The Resistance workers in Zeist also had an exceptional stroke of luck during this difficult period. It turned out that the district Unterkommandant for the Gestapo was not in sympathy with the Nazis. Instead he secretly offered his support to the Dutch resistance. Whenever a *razzia* was imminent, he alerted the activists to the threat. This meant that the Kaans were able to offer fugitives other than Philine the opportunity to *onderduiken* in the hiding place in Louise de Colignyplein 15. Later in the war, the son of a government official from the Dutch East Indies managed to escape from Belsen and find sanctuary with the Kaans for some months. Fred still recalls graphically the young man's shaven head – a sight not often seen at the time.

The *razzias* were highly organised and terrifying for young Fred and Herman. A whole section of the town would be closed off with tanks and lorries, and troops would charge into each house. Those involved were the Brown Shirts, the *Sturmabteilung* (SA) and the Black Shirts, the *Schutzstaffel* (SS). Of these, the SS were the most feared as they worked closely with the Gestapo. The purpose of the *razzias* was not only to search for fugitives, but also to requisition all kinds of goods. These included copper and other metals, blankets and radios. It was during these raids that Fred started to have the first stirrings of the pacifism which was to become central to his adult life. He became aware that not all the soldiers were totally evil and some of them, being conscripts, had not volunteered to fight. They were just fellow human beings with wives and children in Germany. On one occasion a soldier burst into Fred's bedroom and then noticed all his pictures and personal effects. The soldier started to cry and sobbed that he also had a son at home with just the same things scattered around his bedroom.

Although life was hard and dangerous, Fred was able to continue his schooling throughout the years of the

Occupation. In 1941, he passed the entrance exam for the grammar school, the Lyceum, and opted for the A stream. Here he studied Dutch language and literature, English, history, geography, biology, physics, maths, algebra, chemistry and astronomy. He also continued with French, which he had already started at primary school, and later started to learn German. This was compulsory under the regime and very difficult for the teacher who taught German. He was Dutch and hated teaching the language of the enemy.

During the first three years of the Nazi Occupation, school carried on much as before although some of Fred's former friends joined the Hitler Youth. Occasionally scuffles would break out in the classroom. The newly converted Nazis demonstrated their loyalty to the party by turning on their classmates with violence. Once, when anti-German feelings were running high, a Hitler Youth member decided to end the argument by bringing a stick down on a classmate's head with such force that he was severely injured. Fred tried to remain anonymous, but this proved difficult as the Nazis introduced new rules and restrictions at every turn. Fred was an enthusiastic scout before the war and kept his uniform and equipment after membership of all organisations was banned. He continued to wear his scout belt, with its distinctive buckle, to school – very necessary as without it his trousers would have fallen down! One day a boy, younger than Fred and fully attired in Hitler Youth uniform, saw the belt and challenged him. He told Fred to give him the belt as such things were forbidden. Fred – feeling relatively safe as he had two friends with him – refused, stating that he needed it to keep his trousers up. The Nazi boy thought about this for a while but insisted that the belt be given up. Again Fred refused. Eventually after some argument, it was agreed that the belt be cut so that they had half the buckle each. Fred felt that he had scored a moral victory as the belt was no use to the Nazi boy – but he still had to keep his hands in his pockets for the rest of the day!

As the war progressed the Germans took possession of the school building. This meant that regular teaching had to stop and the studies of the more senior students were severely disrupted. However, they were permitted to continue studying with tutors in their own homes and groups of ten students formed classes in private front rooms. In spite of the difficulties and disruptions, this proved to be a very effective way of studying and, to his surprise and delight, Fred achieved very high marks in his leaving diploma.

There were other academic benefits from his unconventional teenage years, including his individual Latin tuition from Philine in the evenings. In 1944, Fred had a bout of very poor health. In the spring and early summer he had acute appendicitis and spent some time in hospital. The operation led to complications and he had to spend several months convalescing. He had only just recovered from this when he contracted scarlet fever. This meant more time in bed. During this period Fred used the German war effort in an interesting way to his personal advantage. Protected by the 'infectious disease' signs, he was able to listen to a crystal radio which had been constructed by his father. He tuned into the so-called 'black' radio stations set up by Josef Goebbels. These pretended to be broadcasts from the British operating behind enemy lines. The most famous of these broadcasters was William Joyce, who became known as 'Lord Haw-Haw' (and was the last person to be hanged for treason). He attempted to demoralise British listeners, starting with the famous catchphrase 'Germany calling, Germany calling'. However, although Goebbel's strategy had some effect on the British, it actually had the opposite effect on Fred! He enjoyed listening and was able to pick up an idiomatic command of English, which was of course to prove invaluable in his later life! The exercise also stood him in good stead at school when his health improved. After the war the class had an enlightened, if very severe, English teacher. He demanded that the pupils listen to the BBC World Service every day. Each morning the teacher would choose a student to summarise world events – in English. Fred's expertise came in very useful as he would listen to the programme early in the morning, write out any relevant points, reproduce them and hand them round the class. In this way, anyone who was less fluent in English, or who had no radio at home, was protected from the wrath of the English teacher!

The last year of the Occupation brought the greatest suffering and sorrow for Fred and his family. The winter of 1944–1945 became known as the 'Hunger Winter' and many Dutch people died of starvation over a period of a few months. The effects of an extremely cold winter were exacerbated by the defeat of the Allied Forces at the battle of Arnhem which provoked a response from the Dutch government in exile. The military plan had been for the British Guards Armoured Division to smash through the German lines and link the bridge at Arnhem with two other strategic bridges at Nijmegen and Grave which had already been secured by the United States Airborne Division. However, although the British managed to take the northern end of the Arnhem Bridge, the Germans, helped by bad weather, managed to retain control of the town and the British were forced to retreat across the Rhine. In September 1944, the Nederlandse Spoorwegen went on strike at the request of the Dutch Government in London in the hope that this would incapacitate the German war machine. All the fuel supplies were in the province of Limburg, the most southerly of the Dutch provinces. This meant that everyone in the three provinces Noord Holland, Zuid Holland and Utrecht had to manage with whatever supplies they had already. In October, by way of reprisal, gas and electricity were shut off except in buildings used by the Germans. The situation brought added danger to the Kaan household because Hermanus undertook the hazardous task of organising payment of salaries to the striking railway workers.

Brandina, though, needed to fight other enemies – hunger and cold. This was because food and fuel quickly became very scarce. In the early hours of the morning Fred and Herman would join neighbours chopping down the trees from the copse opposite the house to burn at home. The timber was cut into small pieces and stacked under their beds. During these months of hardship the only way that food could be obtained was by bartering with farmers in the surrounding area. Brandina was one of the unobtrusive women who would go out into the countryside and exchange items of clothing and jewellery, sometimes for just one piece of bread. Some of the farmers chose to exploit the situation as a business opportunity, but others were more generous. Meal times were very distressing. On one occasion, the whole family had only one slice of bread between them. The arguments over who was going to eat it ended in tears and the meagre ration was shared equally between all four of them. It was considered a delicacy to eat pancakes made from a mixture of mashed potatoes, tulip bulbs and any other more or less edible scraps of food, flavoured with home-made sugar-beet syrup. These pancakes were made and sold by the local baker as there was no flour available. The result was a sweet confection which, although just about edible, was not at all nutritious.

The reason why Brandina was the only family member who could go out to the farms to search for food was that, during this period of the war, life was extremely dangerous for teenage boys and men. The Germans badly needed manpower to build their fortifications along the demarcation line in the provinces of Gelderland and Drente. Officially, all males between the ages of 17 and 40 were required to report for duty. Unofficially, Germans patrolled the streets and rounded up anyone they found out and about. They even raided houses, so Fred, Herman and Hermanus were forced at times to crouch in the hiding place under the stairs.

Eventually, the Red Cross administered a modest aid programme, but even so casualties were very high. Many people died of malnutrition, including three of Fred's grandparents. The people who died could not be buried in wooden coffins as all the wood was needed for fuel. Brandina herself developed oedema and her weight loss was so severe that she received visits from the Red Cross. Although Brandina survived the war without obvious physical disability, the long-term nutritional deprivation led to failing mental health from which she never fully recovered.

Having lived most of his childhood under an oppressive regime, Fred decided that war could never be the answer to the world's problems. During his teens he became a committed pacifist, a path from which he has not since wavered.

# 4

## England 1946–1954

After the war, things returned to some semblance of normality so Fred and his brother began to enjoy life again. They both re-enrolled as boy scouts – an activity that had been forbidden by the Germans during the Occupation. Furthermore, all scout huts had been demolished or taken over by the Nazis. However, after the war a programme was set up by the worldwide scout movement to revitalise scouting in the formerly occupied countries, notably Holland and Belgium. One initiative was that an English scout troop should adopt a Dutch one, and a cultural exchange take place in the form of letters and visits. During the winter of 1946, Fred's company were all encouraged to write to English scouts. Fred, with his growing love of the English language, was more than delighted to take up the challenge and was given the name and address of a fellow scout, Peter Hayward, from South Woodford in Essex. Fred initiated the correspondence and the first letter was delivered to Peter on Christmas Day 1946! This was the start of a long and close friendship which was to be crucial in shaping Fred's future.

Fred became an enthusiastic correspondent, not only with Peter, but with other boy and girl scouts in Europe and the USA. Many of these letters came as a complete surprise to Fred, who had not given out his address to anyone else! In fact, Fred had a fantasy that he might become a famous person in the States. He wrote to Peter:

> When perhaps I go to America lots of girls and boys will be waiting in the harbour to meet that famous Fred Kaan!

Although this, of course, was a joke, Fred's fantasy was to come true, at least in part, and some of those early friendships continue today, fifty years later.

Of course, Dutch young people had had no social life under the Occupation, because dancing and music were forbidden and strict curfews were imposed. Soon after the war, Fred was able to find an outlet for his love of music at last and started a jazz band. Both Fred and his brother played the guitar and their group was called the Scout Serenaders. There were two other guitar players in the band and Fred was the leader. Later the band expanded to include more guitars, a ukulele and some female vocalists. They gave concerts at the local hospital, as well as at school. Fred wrote about his musical success to his penfriend, Peter, and even asked if he could find out the address of a leading ukulele player of the time, George Formby!

Now that the Occupation was over, school became a different place and Fred was able to enjoy learning in a much more relaxed atmosphere. The actual school buildings needed extensive repairs following the mistreatment they had received at the hands of the Nazis. One day in 1946, Fred entered school to be confronted with a beautiful girl with a wonderful suntan. This was Elly Steller, the daughter of second-generation missionaries from the island of Sangir in the Dutch East Indies. Instantly, Fred fell in love with her.

Although Elly had never lived in Holland, she had been repatriated as a Dutch citizen straight after the war. Her wartime experience had been complicated, because Elly's mother had died when she was young and her stepmother, Hedwig Bartels, was German. Although Hedwig could have claimed Dutch nationality as she had a Dutch husband, she chose not to as the capture of Germans seemed to be arbitrary and some managed to escape incarceration for no apparent reason. However, when the Japanese entered Java all foreign nationals were rounded up and Hedwig and Elly's father were sent to separate internment camps. Elly herself managed to avoid this as she was staying with relations in Bandung and was taken by an uncle to a boarding school. Elly's father died of malnutrition in the camp and Hedwig endured great suffering. She emerged feeble and acutely undernourished.

Having been liberated from the camp, Hedwig went to Bandung to join Elly and her other relations. She was suffering from severe oedema and consequently was near the top of the list of those to be repatriated to Holland. Elly and Hedwig had an arduous three-week sea trip, organised by the Dutch government, which took them through the Suez Canal. As Hedwig recovered, the two began to plan for the future. Hedwig had been brought up a Moravian and had even taught music in a Moravian school. It was therefore not altogether surprising that they looked to the Moravian movement for assistance – which is how they ended up in Zeist. At first they had rooms in the *Zusterhuis*, the building set aside for women.

Elly was seventeen when she returned to school. However, she was unable to complete her formal secondary education because she had missed too much during the war as there was no schooling available to her. She completed her first diploma, generally taken when pupils were sixteen, but did not finish the second, for those aged eighteen and above. The day Fred first noticed her was, in fact, her very first day at school. At first, he did not dare speak to her because she was in a higher class, but after he plucked up the courage to approach her they quickly became close and walked to school together every day for the next two years. Elly even started to play the banjo in Fred's jazz band.

It was during the last few months of the war that Fred's interest in religion and the church had started to grow. He began to attend church in Zeist. He quickly became an active member and was invited to join the committee responsible for organising services for young people. He attended confirmation classes at school led by Professor Doctor J. M. van der Linde and became a member of the Netherlands Reformed Church in 1947. Having witnessed the atrocities of the war and endured personal suffering, he found the concept of war, and indeed any kind of oppression, anathema. He confided his pacifist convictions to one of his teachers. The teacher told him to hold fast to his beliefs, and when the two met again many years later at a peace conference in Sweden, Fred could confirm that he had done so! Brandina, his mother, was also drawn to a more spiritual way of life and shortly after the war managed to persuade Hermanus to move from Louise de Colignyplein 15 to the Moravian settlement in Zeist. Here they lived on the corner of the *Broederplein*. For Fred, this was also an introduction to living in an international community, as Moravians from the Dutch East Indies also lived there. For a period of time Fred even shared his large bedroom with a young man called Jaikaran Nath Katwaroo, from Surinam. Fred was able to extend his interest in languages, as Jaikaran taught Fred his native Creole.

Having had his freedom to travel so severely restricted throughout childhood, Fred was desperate to explore more of the world. His correspondence with scouts abroad, as well as his contact with the liberating troops from England and Canada, also made him long to visit new places. Financing journeys in Europe was not actually a problem for the Kaans, since Fred's father had the benefit of free passes from the Nederlandse Spoorwegen. Fred, however, had some difficulty persuading his family to take advantage of these. In the end, though, he managed to convince his parents and brother to plan a trip to Britain. They were particularly interested in this destination because they had become close to some British soldiers and had spent many a happy evening in their company. These soldiers offered the Kaans warm invitations to visit them in Scotland and eventually, in 1947, the family set off for an extended visit. The first place they stayed was a bed and breakfast in South Woodford chosen by the Hayward family. This was followed by a full five weeks in Scotland. Fred still recalls with amusement that summer that year was exceptionally hot and there was even a water shortage. Thus, the Kaans were lulled into the false belief that Scotland was a warm and arid country!

The Hayward family was very welcoming. Peter's father was the secretary of the local Congregational church and Fred found that he was drawn to this free-church denomination with its local autonomy and absence of a written creed. On his return to Holland, he pursued his interest in theology, and felt a calling to be a minister. In order to follow his vocation, he needed to add Greek, Latin and ancient history to his studies which meant that he had to find a private tutor. Fred completed the required courses in two years and took both written and oral examinations at the Ministry of Education in The Hague. He passed these with high grades. By 1949, he had decided to study theology, with psychology as a subsidiary subject, at Utrecht University with a view to becoming a full-time minister. During this period, all young men in Holland were obliged to do National Service, but it transpired that Fred was excused on the grounds of his vocation even though he took and passed the necessary examinations and medical.

University in Holland in the late 1940s presented Fred with some curious paradoxes. He found that the theology department at Utrecht had altered its philosophy very little to accommodate the changes forced on the population from living under the Occupation. Before the war, the Netherlands had been a staunchly Christian country that espoused a strict, traditional moral outlook. University departments were backward looking and maintained a rigid adherence to the conventions of the past. However, the post-war country embraced a more secular view of the world influenced by its recent sufferings. Fred, along with his fellow students, felt compelled to question the old ideals in the light of his new pacifist views. He felt he must face up to questions such as: 'What kind of God would allow such suffering to take place ... ?' Furthermore, there were significant changes for the church internationally. For example, there was the suppression of the Eastern Orthodox Church by the Communists when the iron curtain divided Europe. Within the bubbling cauldron of new ideas were the writings of contemporary theologians such as Dietrich Bonhoeffer and Karl Barth. Bonhoeffer was hanged in 1945 for his part in the assassination plot on Adolf Hitler. In his *Letters and Papers from Prison* he optimistically predicted changes in theology and philosophy in the modern world. These changes were readily embraced by the younger generation of theology students of which Fred was one. It is no wonder, then, that Fred felt restless inside the academic straitjacket of orthodox theology at Utrecht.

In 1949, the same year that he began his studies at Utrecht University, Fred became engaged to Elly Steller. When she had first come to the Netherlands and recommended her education, Elly had set her mind on becoming a journalist. However, she realised that she was going to need other skills and abandoned her plans for a writing career. Instead she enrolled in one of Holland's best-known domestic science colleges in order to prepare herself for the sort of tasks a minister's wife in the 1950s might be expected to undertake.

Fred started to explore many aspects of Christian life in Holland, but found he had more and more sympathy with English Congregationalism. This was because Congregationalists allowed each congregation to manage its own affairs. Congregationalism was established in England in 1580. The Congregational principles were laid down by Robert Browne, hence their original title of 'Brownists'. During the civil war they joined Oliver Cromwell in opposing Charles I. For Fred, there was a church of similar persuasion in Holland called the *Remonstrantse Broederschap*. This denomination was organised on Congregational principles, having no written creed, and each church was run locally by its own hierarchy. However, the *Remonstrantse Broederschap* did not provide Fred with the freedom he sought for his ministry. Furthermore, Fred was influenced by the writings of Karl Barth and especially his article on the subject of Congregationalism in the journal *Die Schrift und die Kirche*.

Peter Hayward's father suggested to Fred that he visit their church in order to assist with pastoral and youth work, and gradually Fred felt called to explore the possibility of serving in the Congregational Church in England. Fred wrote to the Haywards's minister, the Rev. W. S. H. Hallett, for help and guidance. He paid a number of extended visits to the Haywards in the late 1940s and started to think seriously about making England his home after he visited the Festival of Britain in 1951.

Having decided that he was called to pastoral ministry in England, Fred needed to find a college in which to study. After several interviews he was accepted at the Western College, which was part of Bristol University. On 20 October 1952, he arrived there with his suitcase. As the only foreign student, he was given accommodation with a tutor and his wife, the Rev. W. J. and Mrs Downes.

Now twenty-three years old, Fred was able both to as-similate the British way of life and recognise its differences from the continental lifestyle. The England he found in the 1950s was congenial, and many of the characteristics of British society delighted him. The people were polite and Fred admired how they accepted the disciplined system of queuing for food, which was still rationed, and for buses and trains. However, he also recognised that the experience of war had been quite different for the British than for the Dutch and this, he felt, gave rise to a slight element of dull-ness. In spite of shortages, food had been adequate for most British people throughout the war. How different this was to the starving thousands in Holland less than ten years previously! This meant, Fred felt, that British people tended to be less adventurous and rather more staid than those on mainland Europe.

He noticed that the British were reluctant to learn lan-guages, even those of their close neighbours, the French and the Germans, and he discovered that British people, ex-cluding the upper classes, rarely travelled abroad. Fred particularly missed Dutch food, as British cooking was often bland at the time. However, he realised that this was partly the result of rationing. Fred's greatest joy was the English language, which he found versatile and clever. He was charmed by the English sense of humour. The habit he had formed of listening to British radio continued and now he was able to enjoy comedy programmes, which he found highly amusing.

Fred was to become one of a very, very small group of European Congregational Ministers. He quickly made a virtue of being a stranger. Since he was already an accomplished linguist, being able to read and speak both French and German, he was ahead of many of the English students. He had also studied Latin, Greek and ancient history to a high level which, of course, stood him in good stead. The greatest difference he encountered in the British academic world lay in the examination and assessment system. In Holland exam dates were chosen by the candidates when they felt ready to face the ordeal! Students were tested on their own before three professors. They learned the outcome of the examination immediately. In England, on the other hand, he discovered he was required to write an essay every three months, which was taken away to be marked. At first, he felt that this was rather like being at school again and he missed the academic freedom of the European system but later he adjusted to the new demands of the British way.

It was fortunate that Fred was already a fluent English speaker, for he needed this facility during his very first weeks as a theology student in Bristol. In Holland it was accepted that no one would preach a sermon until he had completed his training. In complete contrast, British theology students were expected to preach from a very early stage in their studies. Indeed, on Fred's second Sunday at college, he was sent to a village church to preach. He was amazed and somewhat bewildered. He had never preached a sermon in Dutch, let alone in English! Of course, few of the students had cars at that time so each Sunday morning a line of vehicles would turn up outside the college to collect the fledgling preachers. Much to Fred's relief, most of the churches in the vicinity were small village churches, and it was possible to repeat the sermon.

While Fred was studying, he and Elly conducted a long-distance courtship. Since he still benefited from free rail travel because of his father's job, he was able to return to Holland to stay with the family every academic holiday. Elly herself had no qualms about the prospect of starting a new life as a minister's wife in England. Having completed her domestic science course, she set about further equipping herself for her vocation. Although her first posts after graduating were in childcare in Belgium, she maintained her connection with the Moravian settlement in Zeist. Later, having acquired the necessary clerical skills, she obtained an appointment in the accounts department of the import/export textile company Wees and Weiss in the Moravian settlement. Elly was fully aware, though, that her main stumbling block was going to be her limited knowledge of English. As her schooling had been severely curtailed during the war, her knowledge of the English language was poor. She turned out to be a fast learner, however, and added English to her sound knowledge of German and Indonesian.

At college, Fred was recognised as a linguist of considerable ability and this prompted the London Missionary Society (LMS) to invite him to put his skill to good use. He was asked to join indigenous scholars in the task of translating the Bible into the language of the Gilbert Islands (now known as Kiribati). Fred discussed this opportunity with Elly, who was not opposed to the plan. However, his mother, Brandina was unexpectedly horrified at the prospect and passionately argued that the family had not made so many sacrifices for Fred to end up as a missionary on the other side of the world! She need not have worried. Fred himself was not enthusiastic about the invitation. He argued that, as a newly graduated minister, he needed to acquire at least some basic practical experience of pastoral work before tackling the highly specialised task of translating the Bible into a language he did not even know.

The first opportunity to experience life as a full-time minister came in the final summer of his training when he undertook a three months' assignment in Wotton-under-Edge in Gloucestershire. Even in this Cotswold village, Fred was able to put his linguistic and international experience to good use. A young farmer had fallen in love with a German girl and they planned to marry. However, the girl's family did not speak English, so Fred was asked if he would conduct the service in English *and* German. He carried this off to the satisfaction of all parties.

Another bilingual marriage was celebrated in 1954 – that of Fred and Elly. Although by this time Fred had many friends in England, all his relations lived in Holland so the ceremony took place there, with Fred's tutor, the Rev. W. J. Downes, officiating.

# 5

## Barry 1955–1963

When Fred had completed his training, the moderator of the Welsh Province, along with the college authorities suggested that Fred accept a position as minister to a large Congregational church in Barry, South Wales. This was an interesting idea, as the Welsh congregations were considered by some to be somewhat insular and conventional. They may well have had an inbuilt resistance to anything out of the ordinary – especially to a young, foreign minister. However, Fred's eight years in Barry were to be an extremely fulfilling and successful time in his early career. As a newly qualified minister, he was enthusiastic and full of ideas which he was keen to share with his congregation. The church itself was an imposing building situated in the so-called 'Holy Corner' on the Windsor Road in the centre of Barry – its near neighbours being equally impressive Baptist and Methodist churches. The Congregational Church was one of the larger free churches in Wales and when Fred arrived in Barry there was a congregation of 250 at Windsor Road and a Sunday School of 125. The church was large and well appointed thanks to the generosity of a Captain Murrell. He was a naval officer whose seafaring connections can be seen to this day in the bridge-like design of the pulpit.

In the summer of 1955, Fred and Elly moved into the red-brick manse in Park Road, Barry. On 6 July, Fred was ordained and inducted to the pastorate of Windsor Road Congregational Church. The day before his ordination Fred asked the moderator, Rev. W. Griffith-Jones, what he should wear for the occasion: 'Fred, put on all you've got!' came the reply! Participants in the service included people who had been significant in Fred's journey towards ordination. The prayers were led by Rev. W. S. H. Hallett, from South Woodford Congregational Church with whom Fred had discussed his call to the ministry eight years previously. Rev. W. J. Downes, with whom Fred had lodged during his student years, conducted the 'Charge to the Minister'.

Elly was enthusiastic about their first real married home, and, although they were short of money, the couple decorated it in an individual style. Their taste surprised the dyed-in-the-wool Barry inhabitants. The stairs were painted in vibrant colours – a different shade for each stair! Instead of carpets in the bedrooms there was linoleum, which facilitated the continental habit of mopping the floors every morning. Other Dutch characteristics crept into the house such as the attractive café nets at the window of the shed where Fred carried out his many artistic projects. Fred was an accomplished artist and had considered studying art before he decided to train as a minister. There was a damp cloth on the step outside for visitors to wipe their feet before they entered the house. The garden was neatly kept and boasted an immaculate vegetable plot, which the bare-legged Elly could often be found tending. Elly was very welcoming and young mothers would visit her for coffee and enjoy her excellent cooking. Some things they had never even tasted before such as her delicious choux buns. The house became a hub of activity in the community and, as the years passed, was frequently full of international visitors.

The continental glamour that the young Dutch couple brought to Barry was in many ways the key to Fred's success. Paradoxically, they were welcomed because they were so different. The young people at the church were delighted at the prospect of having a young, handsome foreigner in charge! When the congregation learned they were to have a new minister, it was suggested that a number of the young people put themselves forward for immediate membership of the church because the Sunday School superintendent thought that it would be nice for the new minister to start his work by welcoming new members. This, however, would have horrified Fred had he known, for he was very strict in his preparation of new members, as they later learned. Over the next eight years the young people felt that their horizons were expanding as morally aware Christians in a changing world. Some of the older, more staid, members of the congregation may have had reservations, but the youngsters were carried away with the excitement of the fresh spiritual challenges. At times they even had to remind themselves that Fred was a foreigner because he spoke perfect English without a trace of accent.

Although Fred was a demanding minister, requiring firm commitment from his congregation, he would never ask anything that he was not prepared to do himself. Far from being a passive bystander, he challenged his congregation by participating himself. He never said, 'this is what I want done', he said, 'this is what we are going to do.' For example, when a working party was set up to make some improvements to the kitchen area of the church buildings, Fred joined Ken Jeffery, Vic Walter, Tom Solomon, Baden Powell and Hector Downes in the hard work! Because Fred never hesitated to join in when necessary, he was popular with the young people and the youth groups flourished.

Although Fred was glad to welcome new members, membership brought with it obligations. In general, Fred required that every member had three basic commitments to the church. They should attend services on Sundays, they should attend church meetings which were then held about once a month, and they should carry out another duty in the church such as coffee-making or crèche duty. However, always the socialist, he added the caveat that if a trade union meeting was scheduled for the same time as the church meeting, they should attend the trade union meeting. Fred recognised the importance of a fulfilling social life and introduced a regular 'Family Night' which took place on a Wednesday evening. An upstairs room was used for this ('our own upper room') and, following an instructional session, there were games and singing which Fred, rediscovering the talent of his schooldays, accompanied on his guitar.

Fred encouraged the congregation to focus on mission work and the needs of the wider world. The Congregational Church had strong mission connections and was convinced that the gospel should be proclaimed even to the

smallest communities. Therefore, they carried out missionary work in the south-west Pacific. From 1844 the Congregational Church had chartered ships to visit the islands there
and meet the needs of these remote communities. The ships,
always called *John Williams* after the famous missionary, were
crewed by professional seamen, but carried missionaries.
Money was raised in Sunday Schools for the upkeep of the
mission ships. Children collected ha'pennies and the picture
of a ship on the so-called 'ship ha'penny' came to be the
symbol that everybody recognised. While Fred was at Barry,
the Congregational Church chartered a new ship called
the *John Williams VII*. Some of the young people had the
opportunity to travel to London to visit the ship. It was dedicated on Sunday 2 December 1962, and Janice Morgan was
one of these who had a wonderful day meeting the crew,
who were all from the Ellice Islands. On the following
Sunday, Fred ensured that the whole church learned of her
experiences by encouraging her to give the children's address. Initially she was reluctant to speak in front of so many
people, but he reminded her that she had made the trip on
behalf of the church and so should share it with the church.
Although the need for the *John Williams* ships has been replaced by air travel, we are reminded of their work in Fred's
hymn *The ship of goodwill* written several years later when he
was at the Pilgrim Church, Plymouth. The text reminds us
literally and metaphorically that giving plays a significant
role in the Christian ideal:

> ... let us pray to the Lord of the seas,
> that the ship may be safe in his care,

and that we, young and old, help this vessel to sail
with our giving, our thinking and prayer.

Fred stamped his personality on the church buildings
at Windsor Road, using his artistic talent to brighten the
gloomier parts of the interior. He put up paintings in a previously dark corner and had the idea of making a cornice
over the heating vent and painting it blue to make an attractive display area. At Christmas this was used to exhibit a
papier mâché crib set, of Fred's own making. Today, this
houses the pewter communion set presented to the church
when he left. Some of his ideas were innovative for the 1950s.
For instance, he set up a loudspeaker in the crèche area at
the back of the church so that young mums could enjoy the
service while looking after their babies. He reorganised the
church to include a 'chapel of youth', an area dedicated to
services for young people. To give this important group a
new sense of identity, he moved the Sunday School from
the afternoon to the morning and renamed it the Junior
Church. Fred took an active part in the sessions for children
and young people, which the minister had not done before.
He decorated this 'chapel of youth' with a triptych of his
own design and painting. It was Fred who initiated the re-
moval of the communion rail, which he thought a barrier
between the congregation and the minister during services.
In spite of his warm and active participation in all aspects of
church life, Fred maintained a formal relationship with his
congregation, always addressing them by their surname and
insisting that they called him Mr Kaan. One day, a young
woman met him in the street and told him of the sad news

that her mother had died. He responded by saying 'O, Miss Davies!' She asked him to call her by her first name, Marian, but he refused. After he left Windsor Road, he at last suggested that they call him Fred – but they never could.

Although Fred enjoyed many busy and fulfilling years as minister at Windsor Road, it was not without great sadness too. Everyone in the church was very excited by the news that Elly was expecting her first baby in the spring of 1956. She gave birth to a baby boy at home on 14 April. It delighted the congregation that he was to be given a Welsh name, Geraint. However, it transpired that Elly had come into contact with the rubella virus during the critical first months of her pregnancy and baby Geraint was born with exomphalos, a distressing condition where the intestines are exposed over the epidermis. He was rushed straight to hospital. Many members of the congregation heard the siren as the ambulance hurtled down the road and news of the tragedy quickly travelled round the neighbourhood. Everyone was full of sympathy for the new parents. Doctors operated on Geraint immediately, but he died three weeks later in hospital. Fred and Elly were devastated. Nevertheless, they had reason to be grateful for the kindness of their next-door neighbour Mrs Roberts, who was generous both in sympathy and practical support to the bereaved parents. In spite of their sorrow, Fred and Elly did not abandon their plans for a big family, and Martin was born on 8 April 1957. Mrs Roberts had, by this time, become a staunch family friend. Martin could not say Roberts, and shortened it to Hop. Thus she became known as 'Aunty Hop', a nickname she kept for the next fifty years! Martin was joined by a brother, Peter, on 10 June 1959 and a sister, Christine Alison Elisabeth, always called Alison, born on 17 June 1963, shortly before the family moved to Plymouth. Elly enjoyed domestic life and although she did not take a prominent part in church activities, she supported Fred in all his ventures. She attended the sewing guild, the sisterhood and entertained other young mothers in her home.

As a foreigner, Fred was in an ideal position to raise the congregation's awareness of the world outside Barry. He did this by using shock tactics on occasions. Once, he used a cassette recording of an African Catholic Mass during a service. This was radical for two reasons. First, because no Mass of any kind had ever been heard before by these Welsh Protestants and, secondly, because the recorded Mass was from Africa – far away from their own sheltered community in Wales. One of the many ways that he drew the attention of the congregation to foreign culture was to introduce them to some of the traditions of his native Holland. A regular event was St Nicholas Night, held on a Wednesday evening in early December. St Nicholas, called *Sinterklaas* in Holland, was a fourth-century bishop of Asia Minor noted in early Christian legend for saving storm-tossed sailors, defending young children, and especially for giving generous gifts to the poor. Nicholas was sometimes said to ride through the sky on a horse while delivering gifts. He wore bishop's robes, and was at times accompanied by Black Peter, an elf whose job was to whip naughty children. A few days before the St Nicholas Night party, each church member drew a name out of a hat and had to buy a present and write a poem for that person. On the first occasion Fred took the role of

St Nicholas, and wore a special costume. In subsequent years the part was taken by one of the youth club members, Ken Jeffery. Presents were distributed to the good people, but of course the naughty ones were whipped by Black Peter, a character played by another youngster, Christine Hawkins. They ate spiced shortbread called *Speculaas* and sang 'Here comes St Nicholas'. Fred told them the myths about St Nicholas and how the Dutch celebrated his night. Another occasion when Holland came to Barry was in September 1957 when the church decided, at Fred's suggestion, to hold a Dutch bazaar. This was held in the church hall and Fred painted a backdrop to look like a Dutch town. The young people who were running the stalls even had the afternoon off school to give them time to dress as Dutch children. Other connections with Holland included several trips to Zeist and to Utrecht. These visits were not only enjoyable for them, but also nourished their growing understanding of Christianity's place in the wider world. It was to Fred's delight that two young men, as a result, decided to answer the call to train as ministers.

Fred was very anxious that his congregation should realise the plight of Christians all over the world. Although he was aware that the congregation gave only modestly to overseas work, instead of demanding that they simply give more, Fred developed a strategy of bringing the 'world church' to Barry. He did this by contacting the British Council in Cardiff and asking if students would be willing to visit his church. Until this time the local worshippers in Barry had been quite unaware of the international dimension of the church, so it was quite strange to be confronted with Christians from other countries and cultures. The general pattern for these cross-cultural meetings was that a group of six or seven students would visit Barry and be offered hospitality. After a meal, there would be discussions and a question-and-answer session, which they called a 'Brains Trust' after the popular radio programme. The visitors would talk about their backgrounds and religious experiences, and in this way the Barry congregation was introduced to the worldwide church at first hand.

The visits from the foreign students turned out to be enormously successful and led to exciting developments in the life of the church. BBC Wales heard that a young Dutch minister in Barry was working not only with his local community but was also attracting international visitors. The BBC decided to broadcast some of the international services that Fred had put together with the help of the church and some of the foreign students. The first of these was broadcast on Sunday 5 June 1960. This service, which was held at Pentecost, had a strong international content. When the visitors from Trinidad and Israel were introduced, it was also noted that Fred himself was a foreigner. In his sermon Fred quoted many instances from the Bible where it is made clear that God intended all races to worship together. He drew attention to the lines of the Nicene creed, 'I believe in one Holy Catholic and Apostolic Church' and he went on to explain:

> *Holy* means: set apart, specially chosen for a specific job. *Catholic* means: universal, all-embracing, unlimited. *Apostolic* means: sending and being sent.

He then set the challenge for those present:

> It is this language of love that we, having learnt
> from Jesus Christ, will be able to speak, and we shall
> be understood by all people!

One of the hymns selected for the service was 'In Christ there is no east or west', and the readings were taken by Olive Maynard of Trinidad and Jamal Sakran, a Christian Arab from Bethlehem.

When Fred started forging these international links the aim was not to bring fame to Windsor Road, but to persuade the congregation to give more generously to the world church. Evidence of his success can be found in one of the church's newletters dating from June 1961. Apparently, on Rogation Sunday, Fred had conveyed vividly in his sermon the concern felt by the World Council of Churches for the hungry people in the world. He states that immediately after the service, one of the congregation gave him a cheque for five guineas towards the Freedom from Hunger campaign!

The success of the radio broadcasts quickly led to arrangements for services to be transmitted on BBC television. The first of these was on 16 September 1962. An unusual feature of this service was that instead of the programme starting with a choir procession, as was customary in such productions, the cameras went into the vestry and started by transmitting the prayers. Once more readings were given by people from around the world, including visitors from Cambodia and Nigeria, and the intercessions were divided up between several participants who prayed from the pews. A young person prayed for the elderly, and an old person for the young; a foreigner for the people of Britain and a British person for the whole world. This service met with great acclaim from the general public and after that Fred became famous for his interest in the world church.

Eventually, Fred persuaded the congregation at Windsor Road to share its Christmas service of nine lessons and carols with foreign visitors. Hitherto, participation in this annual service had always been confined to local dignitaries and church officials. Now each reading was read by one of nine students from nine different countries. The result was electrifying. On one occasion Jamal Sakran, a frequent visitor to Barry, read the story of Christ's birth from St Luke's Gospel. Another reading was delivered by a Buddhist woman, Youvin Pou, from Cambodia.

The benefits of these international links were felt across the congregation at Windsor Road. Deep and lasting friendships were forged and everyone became more aware of the wider church. Furthermore, donations to the world church increased without Fred even having to suggest it. Fred remains convinced that it was only after they caught a glimpse of the rich variety of spiritual life throughout the world that the church in Barry really started to blossom. Fred kept a visitors' book and by the time he completed his ministry in Barry, he had signatures from fifty-two countries. Windsor Road continued to hold international services long after Fred had left.

During his time at Windsor Road, Fred not only encouraged the congregation to take an active interest in the world church, but also developed his own contacts. One country which was of particular interest to him was Sweden.

This was partly because one of the Swedish churches, the Swedish Mission Covenant Church, was similar in doctrine to the English Congregational Church and thus was involved in the embryonic discussions working towards unification with other Reformed churches. Fred participated in these talks and was also frequently invited to give lectures to the Swedish Mission Covenant Church. He became fascinated by the language and started to study it seriously. During his visits to Sweden he met an influential church musician and composer, Anders Frostenson, a relationship which was to prove particularly fruitful in later years. Fred was able to develop his links with Sweden to the benefit of the congregation at Windsor Road. In 1956, a group of young people from the Swedish Mission Covenant Church arrived in Barry in order to study English. Their leader, Jan-Erik Wikström, had heard of Fred and decided to make contact with him. The Swedish students were learning English as part of a campaign by the Swedish government to raise the quality of English-speaking in Sweden after the Second World War. The group returned for three or four years and Fred became very friendly with Jan-Erik Wikström, who was later to become a powerful liberal politician in Sweden. In typical Kaan style, Fred gave the visitors a part in the services they attended at Windsor Road, to which they contributed some of their native music. Fred grew interested in Swedish hymns and folk songs as well as the language, a passion he was to return to later on.

Fred had as yet written no hymns. However, his absorption in language and etymology as revealed in his sermons was a sign of what was to come. For example, he had a reputation for choosing the right word or phrase for any occasion. He also encouraged others to write verses and poetry, and held regular competitions for the young people. The hymn book used at Windsor Road was *Congregational Praise*. This had been published in 1951 and so was a relatively recent collection, and Fred used it to introduce the congregation to lots of new hymns. Although *Congregational Praise* reflected the traditional, somewhat backward-looking sentiments of post-war congregations, it seemed to Fred quite modern in outlook. This was because he came from the Dutch Reformed Church, which had little in the way of congregational song. He enjoyed selecting hymns from the whole book, rather than choosing only a few favourites. The church had an accomplished organist and responsive choir. Fred himself attended choir practice regularly – again an example of how he practised what he preached. He declared: 'Worship is what is worthy of God, so we must offer him the very best.' On his last Sunday at Windsor Road, he presented the congregation with something new – his very first hymn! For this he returned to his Dutch roots, offering a translation of a Dutch text by the *Remonstrantse Broederschap* minister, Jan Thomson (1882–1961).

> God calls his people firm to stand,
> with them his work is shared.
> To follow Christ with open mind
> let Christians be prepared.
> We know that they who venture much
> will master earthly strife,
> and they who give and spend themselves
> will gain a fuller life.

God calls, and he provides the grace
to undergird our will;
it gives us confidence that he
can good create from ill.
Beyond each barrier that divides
he shows the vision clear
of new creative human-ness
in every field and sphere.

God calls, and powers that break and part
are void; and all are one,
united in a life of love
together with his Son.
Whate'er across the world may rage,
yet wins his purpose through,
and in each Christ-belonging heart
his reign begins anew!

# 6

## Plymouth 1963–1968

By 1962, Fred had served a full eight years at Windsor Road, Barry. This was four more years than the standard four years expected of Congregational ministers. Although he was happy and still making a rich contribution to the flourishing life of the church, he was starting to feel ready for a new challenge. Later the same year he met Elsie Chamberlain, who came to preach at an anniversary service. Elsie was an influential member of the Congregational Church, having been chairman of the Congregational Union of England and Wales (CUEW) and on the BBC Religious Broadcasting staff. She became friendly with the Kaan family and visited them several times. Her husband, the Revd John Garrington, was an Anglican vicar who also worked voluntarily as a psycho-therapist and hypnotherapist. He held a monthly clinic at the Pilgrim Church in Milehouse, Plymouth. Here, along-side a medical doctor, Emrys Owen, the minister and one of the church elders, he offered assistance to sufferers of chronic illnesses such as asthma.

The Pilgrim Church was an amalgamation of three smaller Congregational churches, Britannia Hall, Sherwell Church and Whitefield Church. Their premises had been destroyed during the Second World War. The congregations agreed to unite in 1947 and, for the next ten years, worshipped in a Nissen hut. Eventually, the opportunity to purchase a suitable site arose and the foundation stone for the new church was laid on 17 January 1959.

During these early years, Pilgrim Church was under the inspiring leadership of the Rev. Ralph L. Ackroyd. He was a determined minister with a modern outlook, and was full of innovative ideas. Rev. Ackroyd undertook responsibility for overseeing the construction of the new church. He favoured an airy and welcoming design to encourage both formal and informal meetings and worship. A large organ was installed and capacious choir stalls stood alongside a huge glass screen etched with symbols of the Christian life such as the vine and branches, the fish and the anchor. Rev. Ackroyd encouraged full participation from his congregation and the church quickly enjoyed a flourishing youth club and Sunday School. In 1963, Ralph Ackroyd responded to a call to minister at Dorking and the position of minister at the Pilgrim Church became vacant. It was Elsie Chamberlain who suggested that Fred Kaan might be a suitable applicant for the position.

In the deep January snow, the Kaan family made their first visit to Plymouth. Fred 'preached with a view' at both the morning and the evening services on this occasion. A few days later, on 31 January, a 'Special Church Meeting' was held to consider the calling of the new minister. Fifty-six members of the congregation were present at the meeting to declare:

> … that this Special Church Meeting sends an en-
> thusiastic and unanimous call to the Revd. Frederik
> Kaan B.A., to become our pastor, to minister to
> the spiritual needs of members and friends and to
> preach the glorious Gospel of Jesus Christ, to spread
> the joy of Christian Fellowship with the Church.

The church had incredible vision and Fred was given every opportunity to experiment with new ways of worship and to develop links with the rest of the city of Plymouth. The church had two mottoes: 'The only tradition we have in this church is that we have no tradition', and: 'In this church everything is possible'. The community which the Pilgrim Church served was socially mixed. The congregation came from the terraced housing up and down both sides of the St Levan Valley which accommodated workers from the dockyard as well as from larger, privately owned houses nearby. There was also an active Junior Church.

Fred's induction service was held on 6 September 1963. The whole family was present including baby Alison, who was then only three months old. Elsie Chamberlain contributed to the service by giving the 'Charge to the Church'.

The Kaan family quickly settled to life in Plymouth. As Alison was only a very young baby when they first moved, Elly did not attend church services regularly but stayed at home with her. Later, when Alison did start Sunday School, she posed a problem for the teachers of the youngest class because she spoke only Dutch! They can still remember the hastily learned phrases to pacify her as she clamoured to join her daddy in church. Martin and Peter both attended a local primary school where Peter in particular revealed a sense of mischief. One summer evening, during a weekly Bible-study group held at the manse, he decided to go out into the road to direct the traffic like a policeman. The meeting was brought to an abrupt halt so that his father could dash out to rescue him. On another occasion, when left in the church kitchen with another little child, Peter brightened up the task of tidying up by having a flour fight. There was flour simply everywhere! As he was being duly reprimanded by his teacher, Fred heard the commotion and wanted to know what had been going on. Poor Peter was in danger of receiving two lectures on his behaviour – one in Dutch, one in English – but the teacher tactfully assured Fred that everything was under control.

The family home in Plymouth was as much a centre for visitors as the house in Barry, where its individual style, including an orange ceiling in the living room, provoked plenty of comment. Even though Fred was absorbed in church business, he still had time to do things with his family. These included regular outings and holidays, often back to Holland. The children and Elly were always included in the various social events for which Fred played his guitar and taught the congregation folk songs.

Fred started to write hymns after only a few weeks at his new post and found himself, quite unwittingly, part of what Erik Routley described as the 'hymn explosion' of the 1960s. Having been given total freedom by the church to explore new ways of worship and service, he suddenly found himself

bored and frustrated by the lack of relevant material in published hymn books. When he first moved to Britain, Fred
was aware of the austerity that was characteristic of the years
which immediately followed the Second World War. In the
late 1940s, there was, in spite of continuing food and fuel
shortages, a strong sense of national pride. However, the pain
and loss of the recent conflict was never far away and this
was reflected in the hymns of the time. Churches were full
and there was a general consensus that the need to maintain
traditions was paramount. Hymns were sung to broad, familiar tunes and the words were often sentimental with a
tinge of nostalgia.

Although the early 1950s were marked by the arrival of
several new hymn books, these were, in many ways, backward looking. *Hymns Ancient & Modern Revised*, *Congregational Praise* and the *BBC Hymn Book* were all published
within twelve months. The *School Hymn Book of the Methodist
Church* (1950) catered for children. Fred had been delighted
initially with the newly published official hymn book of the
Congregational Church, *Congregational Praise* (1951), since it
was so removed from anything he had experienced in the
Dutch Reformed Church. Gradually, however, he came to
find the collection limiting because in common with *Hymns
Ancient & Modern Revised* (1950) and the *BBC Hymn Book*
(1951), most of it had been written twenty or thirty years
before and so the sentiments expressed were not really those
of modern, post-war, Britain. Fred discovered that there were
many areas of contemporary Christian life not covered in
*Congregational Praise*. He sensed a new radicalism in the air
which suggested that the church and its liturgy were no

longer confined in the straitjacket of tradition. Furthermore, Fred also felt the images of the New Testament were metaphors for social concern, something that was also felt by his contemporary Sydney Carter. A specific omission that Fred found in *Congregational Praise* was that worshippers could not make the leap from the intimate act of communion within their own church to the sharing of bread in the wider world. The first hymns, therefore, that Fred wrote were post-communion hymns. Indeed, the very first text he wrote, 'Now let us from this table rise', takes us on the journey from the individual renewal of communion to the challenges of Christian life.

Gradually Fred became a prolific hymn writer. His aim was that the hymns should capture in words and music the full meaning of the sermon as well as other aspects of the service. It became his habit to write a new hymn every week. He wrote these late on Saturday nights and reproduced them in readiness for the services next morning. Early on Sunday morning, the choirmaster and organist, Bernard Warren, would call round to collect the text and to advise on suitable tunes. Bernard was an experienced and exacting musician. The large choir was well trained and used to singing ambitious music including a cantata each Easter. Bernard had strong musical opinions and would not hesitate to make suggestions when the text needed to be altered to fit the tune. All of the tunes were selected from *Congregational Praise* so they were well known to the worshippers. The choir quickly became used to learning texts at short notice and the hymns were invariably well received by the congregation. In time, a large number of texts were amassed and these were typed and reproduced by stencil. Meanwhile, however, Fred's career as a famous hymn writer suffered a setback. When he realised that he had accumulated a large body of texts, he sent some on loose sheets of paper to Erik Routley, a composer and hymn writer who was heavily involved in the 'hymn explosion'. Fred received a very cool response from Erik, who claimed that Fred's texts offered nothing new to hymnody. Although Fred was a little crestfallen, he continued to write texts and eventually put together a printed collection. This was to become the first version of *Pilgrim Praise*, a words only collection of twenty-five hymns. A copy was sent to Erik Routley, who this time responded favourably and indeed promoted some of the texts to hymn-book committees. Although very much an 'in house' publication, *Pilgrim Praise* quickly found its way around the United Kingdom as, in Fred's words, visitors to the Pilgrim Church 'played fast and loose with the eighth commandment' – *thou shalt not steal*! In this first collection of 1967, Fred paid tribute to the help he had received from the Pilgrim congregation as 'both inspiration and sounding-board'. He also declared that the hymns 'do not pretend ... to be anything more than "local praise"'. A second edition, which contained fifty hymns, was produced in the following year and this was sold to other churches for a small profit. Fred made a gift of the book and its proceeds to the Pilgrim Church.

The Pilgrim Church was involved in the social and political life of the city of Plymouth and the congregation was keen that its worship should reflect this. One of the main themes in Fred's ministry was his awareness of Christ in the here-and-now. He felt that the wholeness of God could not be reflected in a divided church or a world in conflict. His search, then, was for unity – both for Christians and for the world as a whole. It seemed to him that the hymns contained in many hardbacked hymn books ignored human needs and desires. He sought to articulate his concern with the church's role in the real world of urban life. Many traditional hymn texts, he felt, ignored everyday problems and were unduly preoccupied with a heavenly wonderland. Such hymns included Felix Adler's text:

> Sing we of the Golden City,
> pictured in the legends old:
> everlasting light shines o'er it,
> wondrous things of it are told.

In response to this Fred wrote:

> Sing we of the modern city,
> scene alike of joy and stress;
> sing we of its nameless people
> in their urban wilderness.

There are many examples of Fred's texts written on specific social and political themes. In December 1966 a 'drama-documentary' was broadcast on BBC television called *Cathy Come Home*. After the screening, the issue of homelessness and how local authorities attempted to deal with it became the subject of fierce public and political debate. (The housing action charity, Shelter, was formed at this time.) *Cathy Come Home* appalled the Pilgrim congregation as it had shocked the rest of the country. In response to the programme, a Shelter group was set up in Plymouth. Fred dedicated to them *A hymn of homelessness*, which focusses on the human side of the nativity. Here is the pregnant Mary denied a place to give birth to the holy child, and modern society, resolutely refusing to learn the lesson, still turns its back on homeless children.

> Forgive us, God, that things are still the same,
> that Christ is homeless under other names;
> still holy fam'lies to our cities come
> where life is sick and sore in crowded slum.

This hymn was introduced at an ecumenical service and members of other churches in the locality attended, including Roman Catholics.

As a pacifist, Fred wrote hymns that were concerned with the struggle for peace. A television programme on Passion Sunday 1966 was broadcast to coincide with the 25th anniversary of the wartime destruction of inner-city Plymouth. Fred wrote a new hymn for this service. In the nave of the bombed remains of the Parish Church of St Andrew's, which still serves as a memorial to the devastation, an apple tree had miraculously grown through the rubble. This symbol of hope inspired Fred to write *The tree springs to life*. The 'tree' of the cross prominent in the first verse 'springs to life' in the last verse, thus restoring us to hope. The tune was also newly composed by the Revd Philip Humphreys.

Fred's most popular text is also concerned with peace. 'For the healing of the nations' was written to mark Human Rights Day in 1965 and has been used on numerous national and international occasions ever since. In this text we are reminded that, with God's help, we must work for peace rather than assume it will materialise out of the blue.

> For the healing of the nations,
> Lord, we pray with one accord,
> for a just and equal sharing
> of the things that earth affords.
> To a life of love in action
> help us rise and pledge our word.

Fred's ideal was, from those early days of hymn writing at Pilgrim, to focus on Christ-among-us sharing our humanity and on justice for all. His uncompromising language attracted criticism of his apparently left-wing message. His *Magnificat Now!* with its confrontational first line 'Sing we a song of high revolt', was included in the early collection of *Pilgrim Praise*. However, a few years later, in 1972, it enjoyed a certain notoriety when concerns were expressed in a House of Commons debate by a Conservative Member of Parliament, Enoch Powell. The hymn was included in the school hymnal *New Life* and a number of parents wrote to Enoch Powell to complain about the hymn. The controversy was further exacerbated by the fact that the text was originally set to TANNENBAUM – a tune associated with the far left and the Socialist song *Keep the Red Flag flying*! The hymn, though, is a contemporary reworking of the Song of Mary – the Magnificat.

Fred used his considerable artistic talents while he was at the Pilgrim Church in much the same way as he had done at Barry. Large expanses of bare brick were decorated with some of his own paintings. He also provided another paper-sculpture nativity.

Fred did not neglect the needs of children in his hymns and the way he used hymns in services. As with his adult

*Fred with his parents,*
*Hermanus and Brandina*

*Fred (left) with his younger brother.*
*The sign says 'from my schooldays'.*

*Fred with his father and brother*

*Hermanus reading*

*Brandina making lace*

*'Dear Brother Scout'*

*Fred in 1947*

*The Dutch bazaar (see page 44)*

*Windsor Road Congregational Church, 'Holy Corner', Barry*

*In council with General Jaruzelski*

*The television preacher*

*Collecting a Th.D.*

*Fred in relaxed mood*

hymns, he wrote the text and fitted it to a well-known tune. Instead of choosing a tune from *Congregational Praise*, though, he selected something children would be sure to know. An early example of this was called *Noah's Ark*, an adaptation of 'The animals went in two by two'. When he first introduced this hymn to the children, they all wore animal headdresses and processed round the church. One of Fred's best-known children's hymns from this period is 'We have a king who rides a donkey', set to the tune WHAT SHALL WE DO WITH THE DRUNKEN SAILOR? Although this hymn is disparaged in *The Hymn Explosion and its Aftermath* by Donald Webster (Royal School of Church Music, 1992), it has been reprinted in countless collections for children since it was first written and remains one of Fred's most well-loved texts. Even Fred was slightly anxious about using such a secular tune, but discussion with a member of the congregation, Kath Hancock, persuaded him that he had 'converted' the tune!

Another means by which Fred accommodated children in his services was to use bold visual aids – unusual for the mid-1960s. One of the ways that he did this was to design and make some lectern 'falls'. These are part of the ecclesiastical decorations used around the church – in this case on the lectern – which are changed in accordance with the liturgical year. Fred introduced these to the congregation by means of a sermon and a hymn written especially for the occasion. He took them through the Christian year, explaining the colours and symbols associated with each season. He writes in his sermon:

> Throughout the centuries the church has made use
> of colours to illustrate the mood of the season; in

this service, too, we use colour together with comment, so that the whole year may come to life. Because that is the intention of course that Christ may
come to life every moment of our days and weeks
and months.

The accompanying hymn, *The colourful year*, takes us on a
journey through the Christian year and explains the reason
why certain colours are associated with each season.

This is how the hymn and the lectern falls work together.

This God who always faithful stays
has given colour to our days.
The shade with which the year begins
is purple: for the people's sins.

On Christmas day we see the light,
– the colour of the feast is white –
and when the Kings have left the scene,
our life runs into days of green.

As red as flames of Pentecost,
so is the blood the martyrs lost.
Then, till the hopeful Advent sound,
we make with green the circle round.

The people of the church are led
through purple, white and green and red,
from fasting days to peaks of feast,
from dark of death to life in Christ.

Fred became quite a famous person while he was in Plymouth. As a result of the televised services, he was asked to present the *Epilogue*, a short programme broadcast every evening before shutdown on the local television channel, Westward Television. For this Fred was required to write five short talks which were broadcast in 1966 under the collective title *Faith for Life*. These talks, later collected into a booklet called *Send Me*, are an interesting look at modern Christianity. Furthermore, they show Fred's ability to take a contemporary expression and apply it to religious life. The titles for the talks were *You're a square*, *To be with it*, *He is way out*, *Playing it by ear* and *This sends me*. This last talk looks closely at hymns and the effect that they have on worship. He talks about a man who ceased to attend church saying, 'the hymns don't send me any longer'. Fred went on to describe the effect popular music had on young people, how there was 'a participation of body and soul' and noted that while they listen to such music they are literally 'miles away'. Perhaps, he goes on, this is what inspired Sydney Carter to write his well-known religious song *Lord of the Dance*, which includes the line:

And I'll lead you all in the Dance, said he.

Fred points out that this echoes the voice calling the prophet Isaiah:

And I heard the voice of the Lord saying, "Whom shall I send and who will go for us?" Then I said, "Here am I! Send me."          *Isaiah* 6:8 (RSV)

As television at that time consisted entirely of live broadcasts, Fred never knew exactly when his programmes would be on. He waited in a room with a bed and had to be ready to leap up and 'perform' at a few minutes' notice. On one occasion, he remembers, there was a general election and his programme was severely delayed. He still had to deliver his talk when all the results were in!

Although Fred had remained at the Pilgrim Church for only five years, this period rewarded him with some of the most inspirational and satisfying experiences of his working life. He not only wrote some of his best-known hymns, but also contributed to the growing ecumenical movement as well as to many social causes. To this day he holds the memory of this time very dear.

# 7

## Geneva 1968–1978

Throughout the 1960s, Fred had been developing his interest in the work of the world church and had become a committee member on the London Missionary Society. He attended the Assembly of the International Congregational Council in Rotterdam in 1961 and a second conference in Swansea in 1966. In the aftermath of the Second World War, fresh thinking on missionary strategy was required and this second conference responded to a report on this subject which stated that the Congregational Church in England and Wales would, with other national unions, be able 'to share fully in the mission of the church so that the gospel is proclaimed to all men, and the church established in every place'. Thus, in May 1966, the Congregational Church in England and Wales, previously called the Congregational Union of England and Wales, was brought into being. In July 1966 the London Missionary Society and the Commonwealth Missionary Society were united under the name of the Congregational Council for World Mission. Fred, with his enthusiasm for mission activities, took a keen interest in the work of Dr Norman Goodall, who had worked for the LMS with responsibility for India and the South Pacific. Following a period of time as Assistant Secretary at the World Council of Churches, Dr Goodall continued his association with the International Congregational Council while in semi-retirement. It was, however, still a surprise to Fred when, in 1968 he received a telephone call inviting him to take up the appointment of Minister-Secretary of the International Congregational Council Executive Committee, to work alongside Dr Goodall in Geneva.

The Congregational Church had been working towards union with the Presbyterian Church since its eighth Assembly held in 1958 and the following twelve years consisted of shared practical and theological work. Fred was considered suitable to undertake this crucial role of Minister-Secretary in the final two years before the union in 1970 because of his gift for making people think in a wider context – an aspect of his ministry that had emerged in his work in Barry and at the Pilgrim Church. Of course, if Fred accepted this position, it would mean leaving the Pilgrim Church. When he first arrived in Plymouth he was asked if he would commit himself to staying for ten years. At the time he felt that this would not be a problem as he had already spent eight fruitful and happy years at Barry, double the usual stay for a Congregational minister. Remembering this early promise to the Pilgrim Church, Fred's initial reaction to the invitation to Geneva was negative. However, he felt it only courteous to mention the matter to the church secretary. He then put the subject out of his mind. He was astonished later to learn that, following his conversation with the secretary, a meeting of the elders and church members was held. Here it was agreed to release Fred.

The family was enthusiastic about the prospective move to Switzerland. The boys, Martin and Peter, looked forward to the challenge of learning new languages and meeting new people. Alison, being younger, had only just started school and took it in her stride. Elly saw the move as part of her role as a minister's wife and her missionary upbringing made it easier for her to accept the upheaval. It was not possible, for financial reasons, for Martin and Peter to attend the International School in Geneva as had first been intended. Instead, they received private tuition in French until they were competent and confident enough to manage on their own. In fact, both boys did very well at school. Although Elly was happy to move to Switzerland, she realised that she would have to add the French language to her newly acquired English. Fortunately, she did not experience too many difficulties as most of her social contacts spoke in English.

The World Council of Churches 'is a fellowship of churches which confess the Lord Jesus Christ as God and Saviour according to the scriptures, and therefore seek to fulfil together their common calling to the glory of the one God, Father, Son and Holy Spirit'. Following rapid expansion after the Second World War, the World Council of Churches abandoned the huts and chalets that had been their home since 1948 and moved into a modern, purpose-built office complex in 1964. The ecumenical enterprises of the church were based here and involved representatives from many traditions and cultural backgrounds. Here each world denomination had its own head and Fred was Minister-Secretary of the International Congregational Council. While he was working in Switzerland, Fred formed a number of close and lasting friendships. The General Secretary of the World Council of Churches, Philip Potter, became a personal friend as did his wife, Doreen, with whom Fred was to collaborate in his hymn writing. It was shortly after the family had moved into their flat in Geneva that Fred answered a knock on the door. The vibrant Jamaican woman who entered was Doreen Potter, a musician who had trained in Liverpool and at Trinity College, London. She announced that she had been writing tunes to Fred's texts and wanted to introduce herself to him. Another colleague was a fellow Dutchman, Albert van den Heuvel, who had studied theology with Fred in Utrecht.

The position in Geneva was both stimulating and challenging for Fred. The first two years were devoted to working towards the unification of the Presbyterian and the Congregational Churches, which finally took place at the Nairobi Assembly in 1970. The two churches were very similar in their doctrine and so it made sense to unite. During the years that Fred was engaged in this project he visited many Congregational churches around the world to discuss the unification. Although happily achieved, the unification meant that there had to be redundancies in the International Congregational Council and the department was reduced to a minimum. Fred was found a new position – Minister-Secretary to the World Alliance of Reformed Churches (WARC). In this role his main responsibility was to oversee the general well-being of a church that had now grown to fifty-five million members. This meant Fred had to undertake an exciting programme of travel and he visited eighty-five countries, some of them many times. For example, he went to Indonesia frequently, visiting member churches in Sumatra and Java, Batak land and Samosir, Bali and its eastward islands, Kilimantan, Irian Jaya … No doubt in part because of Fred's good work the Reformed Church retains a high membership among Indonesian churches to this day.

In 1972 Fred visited Korea in his capacity as Minister-Secretary of the WARC. On this occasion he stayed with a Canadian missionary and his wife. While he was there he happened to glance through a magazine called *The United Church Observer* which was the official publication for the Canadian churches. His attention was drawn to a long article about a church musician called Ron Klusmeier. There was a detailed review of an album that Ron and his wife Chris had recently released. Fred was amazed to read that, of the twelve songs included on the record, ten were arrangements of his texts! As soon as Fred returned to Geneva, he made enquiries about the article and was put in touch with Al Forrest, the magazine's editor. Al was embarrassed that Fred had not been approached for his permission to use the texts and immediately insisted that Fred and Ron meet at the earliest opportunity. In those days Fred's hymns were largely unpublished and he did not expect payment for the use of his texts, but gave them freely to anyone who was interested in using them. At the time, Ron was on an extended concert tour, but Al was most insistent that this was curtailed and sent air tickets for him to travel to the east coast of Canada where he met Fred, who had likewise flown in from Geneva. In spite of the potential awkwardness, the two men got on very well. A collaborative relationship was born and this was to flourish into the new millennium. Ron, as a prolific writer, composed over 600 hymn tunes of which 100 were for Fred's texts.

Fred had three main responsibilities in the WARC. In the area of communications he was editor of the four-language Reformed Press Service and managing editor of their quarterly bulletin *Risk*. *Risk* was launched in 1965 and was, for the time, an exciting new publication expressing many of the emerging ideas and philosophies of the post-war years. In 1977 its title changed to *Youth* and in 1992 it was replaced by a more general publication. Of course, Fred was able to bring to the magazine all his skills and creative flair, which was also expressed in the hymns that were published in it. He continued to write in everyday language, sharing Albert van den Heuvel's view, 'It is dangerous to work for an urban faith and to sing on Sunday about nothing but nature.' Frequently Fred found himself in meetings which he found less than stimulating. Indeed, in one of his hymns, he challenges the validity of these endless discussions:

> While people starve in cities,
> we travel to committees
> until the kingdom come.
> We share a high allegiance,
> divide the world in regions;
> departments are our second home.

Occasionally he would take advantage of an inspirational moment, even during a tedious debate. Such an occasion occurred at the Assembly of the Indonesian Council of Churches in 1976. Fred's colleague, Albert van den Heuvel remarked, 'You know, when you take it down to the basics, all that Christians have in life is a piece of bread, a sip of wine and a song.' Fred, with his inimitable gift for finding the right words, responded to this chance comment with a three-verse hymn. Although called *A minimal hymn* at the suggestion of Philip Potter, the text distils the vastness of the Christian experience into 'a story and a song' and the faith that comes from a 'glimpse' of the Lord. The simplicity of the text stands in telling contrast to the complexity of a spiritual life.

Fred was responsible for the well-being of persecuted Christians in the Middle East, India and the islands of the Pacific. However, he also visited other areas of the world and made countless trips behind the Iron Curtain, especially to Hungary. Here he spent time negotiating with the Minister for Religious Affairs to allow Christian students to spend a year in the West. It was through Fred that many Hungarian students were able to complete their masters' and doctoral degrees by studying at Montpellier University. Fred journeyed to Budapest, which inspired a family interest in Hungary, not least because Elly's earliest traceable forbear was a Hungarian Lutheran minister, who was also a hymn writer! In the seventeenth century, during a period of persecution, all Protestant ministers were made to march to Naples where they were forced to work as galley slaves. Many died during the trek. These Protestants were liberated by

Admiral de Ruiter, and during the 1960s Elly was invited to attend a celebration to mark the tercentenary of their freedom. Fred went with Elly as her guest – the only time during their marriage that Fred found himself playing second fiddle! The Kaan family maintained their connection with Hungary because Peter actually married a Hungarian.

While he was working in Geneva, Fred was encouraged to visit religious centres of all faiths and denominations. This included, on one occasion, a visit to the Vatican. A high-ranking priest took charge of Fred, showing him around all the offices and introducing him to many other members of staff. Towards the end of the visit, they moved outside into the beautifully designed and maintained courtyards. As they turned a corner, the priest drew Fred's attention to a specific spot. 'Look, Fred,' he said, 'this is where we used to burn people like you!' The remark was intended as a joke, but Fred was never so aware of his own Calvinist roots.

During his years in Geneva, Fred wrote hymns for ecumenical and international occasions – often by invitation. One significant project was his contribution to *Cantate Domino*, an ecumenical hymn book compiled under the musical editorship of Erik Routley. *Cantate Domino*, published in 1973, was not entirely a new publication. In fact, it had started life in 1924 as a student hymn book issued under the auspices of the World Student Christian Federation and was widely used for the next fifty years. During this period it was revised and updated several times, notably in 1951. However, even though hymns from all cultures were included, it still seemed impossible to adapt much of the music to a style which would be acceptable to countries with different musical traditions. Eventually, in 1968, it was decided to re-vise *Cantate Domino* completely, and since it had effectively become the hymn book of the World Council of Churches, it seemed appropriate to ask the 1968 Uppsala Assembly of the WCC to take on the responsibility. Thus, the fourth edition of *Cantate Domino* contained songs and hymns from all the main denominations of the Church – Orthodox, Roman Catholic and Protestant – and from a wide variety of cultures. Fred himself had a number of hymns selected for inclusion – thirteen of his own texts and sixteen translations from other languages. Fred also had the opportunity to col-laborate with Doreen Potter on this project.

Whilst *Cantate Domino* was an international and ecumeni-cal hymn book, its focus was essentially western. Towards the end of the 1960s, Christians in Asia realised that there was no contemporary collection of hymns which addressed the needs of non-European urban worshippers. At the Urban and Industrial Mission which met in Calcutta in July 1969, delegates started to sing some of the songs that were com-ing out of the Asian cities. As a result, Professor I-to Loh of Tainan Theological College in Taiwan was asked to edit and make a collection of these songs which was to become *New Songs of Asian Cities.* I-to Loh took leave from his regu-lar pastoral commitments to travel around Asia in order to record original and new songs that were sung by city people. The texts were collected by asking members of the local community to write them down in their own language and dialect. Not all of the songs were explicitly Christian in their language but they were felt to reflect the Christian ideals of modern city life. Neither were all the songs Asian;

some western classic songs of protest were included such as *We shall overcome* and *One man's hands*.

Fred became involved in the project when he was asked to paraphrase into English some of the texts that had come from both Asian and other sources. These included languages as diverse as Ceylonese, Bengali, Marathi, Swedish and Bemba. In order to help make accurate and fluent translations of the songs, Fred had to travel to Jakarta. However, frustratingly, his entire stay was spent in his hotel room listening to tapes and examining texts! Later, the editorial committee met in Jakarta in 1972. The resulting *New Songs of Asian Cities* was an eclectic mix of traditional Asian texts and melodies, alongside popular western hymns and songs of a thought-provoking nature. Some of the tunes were composed especially for this publication. Although Fred found the work arduous, he was pleased to take an active role in the project because so many of his personal ideals were reflected in the contents – those of the needs of Christians in the busy modern world. Indeed, some of his own texts were included, such as 'For the healing of the nations' and *Magnificat Now!* Instead of the traditional European tunes for these words, both of which are also familiar as Christmas carols, new tunes were composed especially to suit Asian ears. The tune for 'For the healing of the nations' was by Sang-so Kwak and *Magnificat Now!* was by I-to Loh. 'Sing we of the modern city' appeared with its new tune by Doreen Potter. Another aspect of the collection that appealed to Fred was the fact that the hymns and songs in *New Songs for Asian Cities* were presented in their original musical form. Generally, the tunes were written in unison, the style preferred in most oriental traditional cultures. I-to Loh expressly stated that he would like the songs to be sung in unison with harmonies added only by guitar chords.

In 1976 Fred and Doreen continued the working relationship established with *Cantate Domino* by collaborating on *Break Not the Circle*, a collection of Fred's texts set to tunes of Doreen's composition. Doreen's simple melodies and harmonic progressions counterbalanced the long lines that Fred favoured in his texts. Indeed, in his foreword to the book, Erik Routley had pointed out the difficulty of setting Fred's texts to music. This is not because of any difficulties in metre, but because the 'combination of delicacy and energy' requires careful handling. Doreen's easy rhythms provided the perfect foil for his words. *Break Not the Circle* was compiled for the Assembly of the World Council of Churches that was held in Nairobi in 1975. Fred and Doreen were determined that the book would be ready in time and managed to complete it in only a few short months. However, the effort was more than worth it because it sold like hot cakes when it went on sale there!

Although Fred's interests and professional commitments took him well beyond European frontiers throughout his time in Geneva, he had maintained his links with Sweden. Following the unification of the Reformed Churches, the ties grew even closer. Early in 1971, Fred received a letter from the secretary of the noted Swedish hymn writer, Anders Frostenson. This was an invitation to translate some of Anders' hymns into English. Fred had continued to study the Swedish language and by this time, he had learned enough to make idiomatic and fluent translations of the texts. Sweden,

along with many other Protestant countries, enjoyed a
revival in hymn writing as a result of the social changes
following the Second World War. These changes occurred
even though the Swedish Church had a strict liturgy and
had hitherto maintained rigid traditions in musical styles
and singing. During the 1960s, a new hymn book was commissioned by the governing body of the Church of Sweden.
Anders Frostenson was one of the best-known contributors,
and he wrote a massive 172 hymns for the book. He had
known Fred since the 1950s and indeed, some of the texts
in this new hymn book were translations of Fred's hymns.
Like Fred's texts, those of Anders proclaimed the presence
of God in the everyday lives of men and women – even in
the cities. Anders introduced Swedish worshippers to the
smell and rush of urban life in much the same way as Fred
had done in 'Sing we of the modern city'. Like Fred he
focussed on the troubled hearts of working men and women
and on environmental issues.

The singing congregations in Sweden have always benefited from the traditions of Protestant music. It was therefore
an exciting cross-cultural exchange when Fred collaborated
with Anders to produce *Songs and Hymns from Sweden* in
1976. This was a collection of Fred's translations into English of texts by Anders and other Swedish hymn writers.
The tunes are all by Scandinavian composers of note such as
Carl Nielsen and Karl-Olof Robertson. The task of translating these texts was demanding as Fred had to travel
to Sweden to carry out the job. However, the trips were
financed by Frostenson, and Fred was delighted to work with
him. Frostenson himself was sometimes an elusive character

to work with as he would frequently disappear on long, solitary walks. These walks would often provide him with the inspiration for a hymn text. On one such occasion he conceived the phrase 'The love of God is broad like beach and meadow'. As he turned these words over in his mind, he carved them in the soft earth alongside a brook. He continued on his walk, but later returned to the same spot where the words were still visible. When he returned home he committed the lines to paper where they became the refrain and opening lines to a four-verse hymn. This hymn is translated by Fred as the second in their collection. Here Anders reminds us of the inclusive love of God who meets us in nature, in our daily sinful lives and ultimately in heaven:

> Your love, O God is broad like beach and meadow,
> wide as the wind, and an eternal home.

During this close association with Sweden Fred came into contact again with Jan-Erik Wikström, the former youth leader whom he had not seen since his days in Barry. By this time Jan-Erik was not only a high-ranking politician but also Chairman of the Deacons' Meeting at Immanuelskyran in Stockholm. Fred was involved in the opening ceremony there in 1974. Fred passed on his love of Sweden and Swedish to his family, especially to his elder son, Martin. Having completed his schooling in Switzerland, Martin became even more interested in languages and spent a year in Berlin perfecting his German. He then went on to study at Hull University in England. As part of his studies he was required to learn another language and decided on Swedish. He went to Umeå, the most northerly university in Sweden, because he did not want to meet any other English students. While he was there, he joined the Swedish Covenant Church, which has a very strong musical tradition. He met a young violinist, Ingmarie, and fell in love with her. They married in Stockholm in 1982 after Martin had completed his Postgraduate Certificate in Education (PGCE) at Keele University in Britain. The ceremony was held at Immanuelskyran, Stockholm, the very church Fred had 'helped open' eight years previously!

# 8

## West Midlands 1978–1985

Just as a surprise telephone call had summoned Fred to Geneva, once again a call out of the blue, in 1978, offered him the opportunity to return to work in England. He was invited to serve as moderator of the West Midlands Province of the United Reformed Church. Initially, Fred did not greet this proposal with great enthusiasm – mostly because the telephone call came in the middle of the night, the time difference being forgotten, and Fred was recovering from a particularly lively social engagement! Furthermore, he felt that, since he had been living away from the United Kingdom for ten years, those who had suggested this appointment knew little of his theology and philosophy. However, the committee that had contacted him was so keen for him to take up the appointment that he finally agreed to come and explore the proposal in detail, before making a final decision. At length, Fred decided to accept the appointment and the family left Geneva for the Warwickshire town of Kenilworth, at that time officially the most expensive area in England!

In the United Reformed Church (URC), the position of moderator is a termed appointment of seven years with the option of a five years' extension. Generally, the URC is in favour of limiting the time any one person can serve in a given post because it ensures that positions of responsibility are not confined to too small a number of people. Fred found the job of moderator extremely exacting because of the diverse roles he had to play. Although he had the opportunity to serve as a minister by taking services and preaching, he was not linked to a specific church of his own. This meant that he could not build the special relationships within one community that he had found so rewarding previously. One of the moderator's principal responsibilities was to look after the well-being of ministers and their families. He was a 'minister's minister'. A moderator was expected to offer special support to churches in crisis, especially when there was a vacancy for a minister. A further aspect of the post was to take the lead among his ministers as well as to preach and lead worship when the opportunity arose. In the URC, at the time when Fred was moderator, the church was divided into twelve synods, each served by a moderator. In Fred's area, the Midlands, he had 166 ministers and 120 churches in his care. The pastoral, administrative and preaching responsibilities were vast, and, taking travelling into account, it meant that Fred worked long days, leaving early in the morning and not returning until late in the evening. He continued to be an extremely active preacher, often preaching as many as three times on a Sunday. It was, however, acceptable to use the same sermon on more than one occasion! The job, then, was very hard work and for Fred it was sometimes frustrating as there was little opportunity for him to use his creative talents. Fred's natural flair for innovation was hampered by the fact that a moderator's assistant had already been in place for some years and had developed his own working style. This meant that, for the first few years, Fred did not have an entirely free hand to establish himself.

The new appointment, however, presented huge compensations for Fred – not least in the close friendships he formed with other moderators. It transpired that two of his colleagues, John Slow and Tony Burnham, shared his passion for jazz. All the moderators met monthly in London and the three would always stay in the same, rather seedy, hotel. In the evening, after a gruelling day of meetings, they would visit either Ronnie Scott's Jazz Club or Pizza on the Park. At Ronnie Scott's they enjoyed music by some of the world's finest jazz musicians and became personally known to some of them. At Pizza on the Park Fred would engage new singer-songwriters in conversation, absorbing details about the music business and sharing experiences about writing lyrics. One of the performers Fred was most drawn to was the jazz pianist Dave Frishberg, whose witty lyrics particularly appealed to him. At the time Frishberg came over from the USA about once a year and Fred, Tony and John made a point of going to hear him. After the evening's entertainment, the trio would return to the hotel on foot. Fred absolutely detested walking and would moan for the entire journey. John and Tony had virtually to frogmarch him home every time!

In spite of the necessary limitations which the position imposed upon Fred, he was able to bring variety and a fresh approach in the shape of his international connections. He conceived the idea that all moderators should visit overseas churches to enrich their knowledge and understanding of the world church. Initially, not all of them were in favour of the plan, but after a period of time, the trips were acknowledged to be a valuable learning and social experience for the whole team. The first of these trips was a return to Geneva where Fred introduced his new colleagues to his former associates at the World Council of Churches. The experience opened doors for the other moderators, and they benefited from contact with people who could give them a different perspective on their work. They also visited Hungary where Fred had recently received an honorary Th.D. from the Reformed Theological Academy at Debrecen in recognition of his work in the field of hymnody and ecumenical relations.

An important feature of these trips was that wives were encouraged to go as well. At that time, all the moderators were male, although this imbalance has now been partly redressed. Many of the moderators' wives felt isolated owing to the very nature of their husbands' work and some felt that they could make a valuable contribution, were a suitable role to be found for them. Travelling alongside their husbands gave the women an opportunity to explore and develop their own ideas and actively contribute to the learning experience. Altogether, to be travelling in a mixed party was a fresh and exciting approach. Fred was always smartly turned out throughout these trips, and the secret turned out to be the travelling iron that Elly always took with her. Once this became known, other wives used to borrow the iron to avoid their husbands looking like tramps when seen along-side Fred!

In spite of the heavy workload of his position, Fred still pursued his active support for persecuted minorities whatever their beliefs. In May 1982 he was invited to join an official fact-finding visit to Poland at a very difficult time in the country's history. In December 1981, the recently formed trade union Solidarity had been declared illegal with the declaration of martial law, and the Soviet Union had replaced Communist Party rule with that of the army under the leadership of General Wojciech Jaruzelski. A group of four representatives from different cultural backgrounds had been given permission to visit Poland. Fred represented the Free Churches. The other members of the group were a Greek Orthodox priest, a Lutheran minister, and an Indian layman. In Poland, life was particularly difficult for Protestants and those of faiths other than Christianity, and this suffering concerned the World Council of Churches. In contrast, Roman Catholicism was tolerated by Jaruzelski, not only because of its influential position within Polish society, but also because of the international prestige of Pope John Paul II, who, before his elevation to the papacy in 1978 had been Archbishop of Kraków. The trip proved to be more successful than any of the four visitors imagined possible. To overcome severe restrictions on air travel to and from the West, they flew from England to neutral Switzerland and from there to Warsaw. They had been assured that their presence would only be tolerated by General Jaruzelski and that he would take no official notice of their visit. However, when the group arrived at their hotel they received a message saying that the General would be willing to grant them an audience of a few minutes. These 'few minutes' stretched to over two hours and they discussed in depth the plight of the minority groups. The result was that Jaruzelski ended up not only supporting their visit, but also providing military transport around the country. Thus they enjoyed unhindered access to all their planned destinations.

While he was moderator, Fred continued to develop his personal style of hymn writing. He had always felt that hymns should reflect every aspect of worship and their 'message' should certainly not be restricted to illustrating the text of the sermon. Indeed, he often remarked that any worshipper should be able to grasp the underlying theme of a service by looking at the hymn board alone. When interviewed by *The Hymn* in October 1980, he said: 'It isn't just the sermon that determines the theme and choice of hymnic material but everything that goes before it and comes after it.' That hymns should be an integral part of worship was further stressed when he warned that careful thought be given to the way in which they were announced. The standard practice of introducing them by number and first line alone should be avoided. The texts Fred wrote during his time as moderator reveal his unease at the way some churches went through the motions of celebrating religious festivals without thought or imagination. *An uneasy carol* overtly reminds us of the need to approach the Nativity with a fresh mind every year:

> Then free us from traditions that diminish
> the glory of your Christmas to a farce;
> make good our will, from yearly start to finish
> to 'see this thing that (daily!) comes to pass'.

As moderator, Fred brought his special creative flair to leading worship at meetings for his fellow moderators. At that time the Synod – when ministers and representatives of all the churches belonging to the Synod met for a day – took place twice each year. Fred would often contribute new hymns for these events.

In the early 1980s Fred's writing career took an unexpected turn when he was telephoned by one of Norway's leading composers, Knut Nystedt. He asked Fred if he was willing to enter into an author–composer partnership with him in the creation of new choral music for choirs and orchestras worldwide. Knut Nystedt was born in Oslo in 1915 and grew to be an influential composer in Norway. Many of his works reflect his commitment to peace and justice, so it was entirely appropriate that the first collaboration between the two was a setting of Fred's *A hymn on human rights* ('For the healing of the nations'). This was arranged for mixed chorus, organ and percussion and was the centrepiece of a new cantata, *A Hymn of Human Rights*, for Human Rights Day, commissioned by a leading university choir on the USA's west coast. The work was published in 1982 as Knut's opus 95. Two years later they collaborated again with the cantata *For a Small Planet* for mixed chorus, string quartet, harp and narrator.

Fred's reputation as a hymn writer who places the modern world and its problems at the heart of his texts was increasingly assured. In 1983, he was one of five international hymn writers to be invited by the American Lutheran Church to mark the 500th anniversary of Martin Luther's birth and baptism with a new hymn. The theme was 'the joy of worship/witness as related to the arts'. Fred's contribution was premiered at a Festival of Worship and Witness in Minneapolis in June 1983. In this text he freely celebrates all the varied musical influences that make worship a complete experience.

> We raise the roof of cellar and cathedral
> with sounds of jazz, with symphony and song,
> and pray that in our practice and our playing
> the consonance with heaven may be strong.

Further acknowledgement of Fred's authority on the subject of hymnody came in 1984 when he was awarded a Ph.D. in Religious Studies by Geneva Theological College in North Carolina for his dissertation entitled *Emerging Language in Hymnody*.

Fred demonstrated his commitment to his pastoral and ministerial duties when, in 1984, he refused to let his name go forward for renomination for a further term as moderator. He was, he declared, committed to 'servant-leadership': he wanted to work closely with his own congregation rather than function as a remote administrator and was anxious to prove this by being open to new and fresh challenges. The following year saw the publication of the most comprehensive collection of his hymns, *The Hymn Texts of Fred Kaan*, for which he wrote an extended introduction developing his ideas about hymn writing and the influences which had shaped his writing.

# 9

## Swindon 1986–1989

At the end of seven years, Fred decided to discontinue his work as moderator of the West Midlands Province of the United Reformed Church. Seven years was the accepted duration of such an appointment but this could be extended for a further five years by invitation. However, Fred requested that he conclude his ministry as he started it – as a minister in a local church. It was fortunate that a timely vacancy arose in the flourishing team ministry at Central Church, Swindon. Fred, with his vast ecumenical experience, was considered to be suitable for the position and was invited to apply.

Swindon, as a rapidly expanding new town, at this time was in the process of change. During the 1960s church rolls declined, and with extensive inner-city development it seemed that the various denominations would do better to work together rather than face extinction apart. Some of the town's Nonconformist churches already enjoyed a close relationship and they agreed to develop yet closer links. In 1970 the Swindon Churches Commission issued a green paper entitled 'A call to the churches in the centre of Swindon'. It emphasised that unity was not simply an ideal but was necessary to prevent wasting resources, for example churches that were half empty yet expensive to maintain.

The plan was to set up a new centre led by an ecumenical team of ministers who would act not only as pastors but also specialise in new forms of ministry and mission. Since none of the existing churches was entirely suitable, the Swindon Churches Commission decided to erect a completely new building. The journey towards ecumenism started, and difficulties over matters of baptism and communion were discussed in full and resolved. Eventually, in 1978, a special service was held with 450 members who signed a common roll, and Swindon Central Church at last began to establish itself. Financing and purchasing land for the site of the new building, however, proved to be a problem and Swindon Central Church spent the first ten years of its existence in the buildings of Trinity Presbyterian Church, Victoria Road.

During the early 1980s Swindon Central Church developed its ministry through contact with branches of the world church as well as initiatives in Swindon itself. It was into this exciting and flourishing community that Fred moved in 1985. The commitment of the Central Church both to the world and the local community suited his passionate social concerns. When Fred was appointed as one of four team members to the Central Church, the new building was still not completed although construction was well under way. He was seen as a bridge between the old church and the new and it was hoped that he would lead the church in this exciting phase of its development.

Although primarily a team pastor at Central Church, Fred was also appointed as sole minister at Penhill United Reformed Church. This was a very small church on a large housing estate. The church had only twelve members. The appointment at Penhill was part-time and Fred was committed to one Sunday service per month and half a day a week for pastoral care. Despite this, Fred was adamant that the 'call' must come as much from Penhill as from the Central Church which meant that both churches must respond to his 'call' equally. Penhill housing estate was vast and, along with several other large estates in Swindon, was originally built to accommodate London overflow families immediately after the war. Each of these estates was supposed to have one Nonconformist church and the Congregational Church, as it was then, sponsored the first of these at Penhill. A committee was formed from members of two other churches, Stamford Street and Emmanuel Church, and an outpost church was established. Initially they held services in an upstairs room at the health clinic, housed in the original farmhouse of Penhill Farm, after which the estate was named. The experiment to have one Nonconformist church serving a large community was not entirely successful, because Methodists and Baptists preferred to worship in their own churches.

Fred first visited Swindon in October 1985 and 'preached with a view' at the morning service at the Central Church and the evening service at Penhill URC on Sunday 27 October. In his sermon he quoted from a hymn that he had written only a few days previously while on a train journey – the 7.40 Coventry to Euston. This hymn, 'Were the world to end tomorrow', reminds us of the need to carry out our Christian duty in the knowledge that the fruits of our actions will benefit future generations, whatever our fears for today.

> Were the world to end tomorrow,
> would we plant a tree today?
> Would we till the soil of loving,
> kneel to work and rise to pray?

The inspiration behind this hymn, Fred explained, came from Martin Luther. He was once asked how he would spend today if he knew that the world would come to an end the next day. Luther replied that he would plant an apple tree. In the final verse of the hymn there is a vision of a truly united and ecumenical church working together with a common aim.

> Pray that at the end of living,
> of philosophies and creeds,
> God will find the people busy
> planting trees and sowing seeds.

The very last line of this hymn was used as the title for Fred's collection of hymns published a few years later in 1989.

While Fred's 'call' to the Central Church was still under discussion, he remained active as Chairman of the Council for World Mission (CWM). Although this was considered to be in tune with the ideals of the Central Church, concerns were voiced that his national and international commitments might keep him from Swindon for long periods of time. These fears, however, turned out to be groundless as Fred was able to assure them that there would be no conflict of interest. Furthermore, with his contacts abroad, he was able to nurture their embryonic connections with the world church. Fred was already known in Swindon as a hymn writer. It was serendipitous that on the very day his acceptance of the dual appointment was announced, one of his hymns, 'We utter our cry: that peace may prevail', was broadcast in a BBC *Songs of Praise* programme.

An 'Act of Worship including The Induction of Fred Kaan to the Team Ministry of Central Church, Swindon and the Pastorate of Penhill United Reformed Church' was held on Saturday 18 January 1986. This service demonstrated Fred's connection with the world church and his commitment to the ecumenical movement. For example, the sermon was preached by the Revd Dr Christopher Duraisingh, the eminent theologian and ecumenist from India. Two of Fred's own hymns were included in the service. The first was a new text, *Round-table church*. This hymn had only just made it into the recently published *The Hymn Texts of Fred Kaan*. Indeed, in this book it appears as a facsimile of Fred's own handwriting at the front of the book. This text was particularly suitable for Fred's induction and to the vision of the Central Church. It was inspired by a poem of Chuck Lathrop and uses a non-Christian image, a round table, to illustrate the concept of Christian fellowship.

> The church is like a table,
> a table that is round.
> It has no sides or corners,
> no first or last, no honours;
> here people are in one-ness
> and love together bound.

*Round-table church* was to prove significant for the Central Church when it finally moved into its new premises in the Pilgrim Centre. With the idea of an egalitarian round table in mind, they chose an oval communion table – no corners, no suggestion of precedence.

> The church is like a table,
> a table for a feast
> to celebrate the healing
> of all excluded-feeling,
> (while Christ is serving, kneeling,
> a towel around his waist).

Another curious fact about *Round-table church* is that, like 'Were the world to end tomorrow', it was also written on the 7.40 Coventry to Euston! *Round-table church* was later included in the collection *Planting Trees and Sowing Seeds*. The Central Church was delighted to have a hymn writer in its midst. Copies of *The Hymns Texts of Fred Kaan*, which had been published shortly before Fred moved to Swindon, were on sale at the church bookstall.

The service to welcome Fred officially to Penhill URC was held the following Sunday, 26 January 1986. This small congregation of twelve members had been without its own minister for over five years. They were delighted at Fred's arrival even though he was to be shared with the Central Church. Fred and his family did not live on the estate but he quickly set about making himself known in the area. He wanted to strike the right balance between ministering to the needs of church members and serving other people on the estate. He did this by visiting schools to take assemblies, joining in with local activities, and meeting doctors and social workers. During his time at Penhill URC, Fred continued to emphasise his commitment to the world church by developing links with Tearfund, a leading relief and development charity, working in partnership with Christian agencies and churches worldwide to tackle the causes and effects of poverty. Fred was also concerned with developing the role of young people in the church. Penhill had its own scout and guide troops, both of which were flourishing under the leadership of Mr Albert Roberts and his wife, Gladys. At one church parade, all the young participants formed a circle around Fred and he distributed communion to them even though this raised a few eyebrows.

Although the congregation of Penhill URC was small, there were still plenty of opportunities both for adults and young people to meet during the week. Membership was fluid as many young professionals started their careers living on the Penhill estate before moving to more prestigious addresses elsewhere in Swindon. Stalwarts such as Mr and Mrs Roberts, though, were loyal in their service to the church and the community. Theirs had been one of the first families to move from east London into a well-appointed three-bedroom terraced house on the Penhill estate. They were delighted with their new home and set about immersing themselves in the community. They recruited scouts and guides for their respective companies, both of which celebrated their golden anniversaries in 2005. Mrs Roberts had been a keen church musician in her youth. During the war she worked in a clerical capacity for the Presbyterian Church in central London. Tragically, on the day of a large meeting a bomb exploded killing all of the occupants of the building except Mrs Roberts. The disaster would have been even greater, had not a number of visiting ministers been delayed by the air raid. Mrs Roberts was very badly injured and her right arm was severed. Pioneering surgery managed to re-attach her arm but she did not regain full use of her hand. However, Gladys would not hear of giving up the piano and gradually developed a special technique to overcome her problem. Eventually, as her confidence grew, she played regularly for church services. Fred worked closely with Gladys to develop hymn singing at Penhill and encouraged her in her playing.

The congregation at Penhill was delighted in 1987 when Fred wrote a new hymn for Mothering Sunday. The tune, PENHILL, was composed by Pamela Ward. The hymn, 'God of Eve and God of Mary', was one of seven runners-up in a hymn-writing competition organised by BBC television. This hymn embodied some of Fred's feminist theology which emphasised the way in which God encompasses the full range of human qualities, feminine as well as masculine. Fred was always on hand to discuss hymn choices with Gladys and became a regular visitor to the Roberts's home. When Gladys became ill in 1987, Fred offered support to the family as she stoically continued to play for services. On Christmas Eve, she finally admitted that she was too weak to deliver her regular reading. She died a few days later, between Christmas and New Year. Planning the funeral posed significant problems and, during this difficult time, Fred showed how much he cared for members of his congregations. Because of the seasonal bank holidays, it was very difficult to make a booking at the crematorium. Fred was already committed to speak at a conference the following week. Eventually, he went out of his way to rearrange his schedule so that he was able to conduct Gladys's funeral – an arrangement that meant a lot to her family. A few weeks later, at the church meeting on 28 January 1988, Fred paid a warm tribute to Gladys's contribution to the musical life at Penhill URC.

Fred and Elly moved into a newly built manse in, funnily enough, Windsor Road, Swindon. The house was rather inconvenient in design with lots of small rooms rather than a few bigger reception rooms. This meant that holding meetings was sometimes difficult. On one occasion all the available space was used and people even had to perch on the stairs!

Even as the prospect of moving to the new church building came ever closer, Fred still used his vision and artistic talent to develop the old church. A prayer chapel was set up at the back of the building to give worshippers a quiet place for personal devotions. The chapel was also used for early morning prayers. As he had done in Barry and Plymouth, Fred brought a connection with his early life to the Central Church by presenting them with a Moravian star. The 26-pointed star was originally used in Moravian schools as a geometry exercise. Since then it has been used by missionaries all over the world and has become a symbol of Christian unity.

Being Chairman of the Council for World Mission (CWM) meant that Fred had access to a vast international network. He shared his experiences abroad with the congregations in Swindon both in his preaching and in his regular contributions to the church paper, *The Spokesman*. The

CWM was, at that time, a partnership of twenty-eight churches in twenty-one countries. The post of Chairman was a fixed-term appointment for two years, with the possibility of an extension for a further two years. In 1987, Fred was re-elected in Hong Kong. He continued his travels, crossing continents to venues as different as Madagascar and Wales! One adventure that he had in Madagascar was a chance encounter with Tony Burnham, a former colleague from his Midland moderator days. Tony, who was on sabbatical, was visiting a Lutheran compound, and he and Fred met up for an evening's socialising. They stayed out so late that Tony found that he was locked out of the compound and had to scramble over the barbed-wire fence. Then he had to race to his room to avoid being caught by the guard dogs running loose!

A year later, in New Guinea, Fred gave the keynote address at a CWM conference and wrote about this experience in *The Spokesman*. Using for his text, 'Ye must be doers of the truth', Fred likened delivering such an important speech to making New Year's resolutions. He reminded Christians of their responsibilities in all areas of their lives. In late August 1988 Fred made an additional trip abroad, leading a CWM visit to the Presbyterian Church of South Korea. Once more, he wrote about what he had learned there in *The Spokesman* and introduced readers to the theology of *minjung* (*min* = people and *jung* = masses) – the theology of the oppressed Korean Church. In Korea, Fred explained, the masses are the farm workers, beggars, slaves and even prostitutes – all trying to understand the gospel in terms of their everyday lives. He wrote:

> What we need desperately is a *minjung* theology
> that will outstrip the niceties and trivialities of so
> much that passes for theology in our churches. We
> need a theology that will cut through ecumenical
> feet-dragging and tiresome dead-end debates in
> synods and assemblies.
>
> *The Spokesman*, November 1988

Fred's interest in feminist theology developed and deepened. He discussed this in some detail in *The Spokesman* and
also started to alter some of his early hymns so that the importance of women as well as of men finds expression. In
*The Spokesman* in June 1988, he lists twelve 'theses' on feminist theology intended to empower women to challenge what
he saw as the oppressive structures in the male-dominated
global community. He offered some examples of inclusive
hymnody, notably *A hymn for Mothering Sunday*, to the tune
PENHILL where he reminds us of the significance of women
throughout the Bible. He links father–God with mother–
earth and suggests that 'the Church, our Mother' is part of
our essential Christian family.

> God of Eve and God of Mary,
> Christ our brother, human Son,
> Spirit, caring like a Mother,
> take our love and make us one!

Fred also collaborated with writers and musicians who
were serving with him at the Central Church. In particular,
he encouraged the Baptist minister, Christopher Ellis, to
write hymns, and one of his early texts was *Abraham and
Sarah*, which was sung at the tenth anniversary service of

the Central Church. Music for some of these hymns was composed by other members of the team, including John Garside, who was one of the organists and the church staffing officer. He composed the tune KAIROS for Fred's text *A time-warp hymn*. Both hymn and tune appear as the first item in the collection *Planting Trees and Sowing Seeds*.

The last article that Fred wrote for *The Spokesman* reflected his developing thoughts about ecumenism and unity. Whilst he had always striven for unity between the Christian denominations, now he recognised that, with the new awareness of the planet's needs, Christians should be prepared to unite for the good of all humanity beyond religious affiliations.

> Humanity is struggling for survival amid dwindling resources and the rapaciousness of rich nations, the nuclear arms race and the common denial of human rights. Is church unity, as we have sought it, enough?
>
> *The Spokesman*, January 1989

He writes that the Christian Church, as a microcosm of society, should be prepared to 'transcend' the ecumenical ideal in an aspiration towards human unity. These were the seeds of thoughts that were to blossom in his later hymn writing.

# 10

## Birmingham and the Lake District
## 1989 – 2005

Although Fred's four-year stay at Swindon Central Church and at Penhill URC was hectic and challenging, it was also very rewarding. During this time, Fred entered a period of self-searching and an urge for change began to make itself felt. Furthermore, a strong and creative relationship started to grow between Fred and a medical doctor, Anthea Cooke. Anthea played an active role in the United Reformed Church and, prior to working as a partner at an inner-city medical centre in a large multi-racial part of Birmingham, had worked with refugees and in hospitals in Madras, India. On her return to England, Anthea became involved not only in GP practice, but also in church-related activities, serving the URC as the medical advisor for candidates applying for the ministry. She devoted a large proportion of her time and skill to caring for HIV and AIDS sufferers and undertook training in psychotherapy. Anthea counselled at Carrs Lane Counselling Centre, a focus for this work in the middle of Birmingham. For a number of years, Fred had been feeling that he and Elly were drifting apart – a sad fact for which he does not seek to deny his responsibility. These changes in Fred's personal life prompted him to offer his resignation as a minister of his pastorate and church in 1989. He left the manse in Swindon and moved to share a new life with Anthea in Hazelwood Road in Acocks Green, Birmingham. The United Reformed Church provided Elly with a house for the rest of her life, and Fred took full care of her financial security. Sadly, after four years of separation, during which time she took an active part in the life and worship of Swindon Central Church, Elly became ill and died of cancer in 1993. A year after Elly's death, Anthea and Fred were married in Birmingham Cathedral, on 2 July 1994. The service was conducted by the Revd Dr Maureen Palmer, one of the first women to be ordained to the priesthood in the Church of England. Some 300 people – several from other countries – were present at the marriage service.

Although Fred was no longer working as a URC minister, he still received a wealth of invitations to conduct services which, of course, he could not accept because he was no longer on the roll of ministers. Eventually, the moderator was approached by the people who wanted Fred to preach, urging him to reinstate Fred as a minister. After two committee meetings permission was granted and Fred was returned to the official list of URC preachers.

The next five years saw a blossoming of Fred's hymn-writing career. One exciting development was his renewed collaboration with Knut Nystedt, the celebrated Norwegian composer. Their first joint work for seven years was *Ave Christe* which was premiered in Ulm Cathedral, Germany in 1991. This was followed by a commission in 1994 from

Save the Children for a piece to commemorate their 75th anniversary in the Nordic countries – that is, Norway, Sweden, Denmark, Finland and Iceland. Fred chose as his inspiration a quotation from Black Elk, a holy man of the Oglala Sioux nation. The result was *One Mighty Flowering Tree*, scored for chorus, brass and percussion. Fred's intention was to make the work not specifically Christian, but to express the holistic philosophy that all humanity should be joined in a deep kinship transcending race and religion. The theistic quotation, used by Black Elk when he was nine years old, uses a spreading tree to represent the aspiration that people 'must live together like one being':

> And I saw all things in the spirit ... and I saw in
> the centre growing one mighty flowering tree to
> shelter all the children. And I saw that it was holy.

The last verse of *One Mighty Flowering Tree*, subsequently called *Imagination is a tree*, urges us to imagine a life where everyone is united in a common desire for peace.

> The scene: imagination is a tree,
> its roots in-earthed, its branches reaching out.
> Imagine life as it is meant to be!
> Make people whole, bring peace on earth about!
> The scene is set, above, below;
> this is the only earth we know.

The culmination of this joint project was its simultaneous premiere on 7 May 1994 in fourteen cities in Denmark, Iceland, Norway and Sweden.

All this time, Fred's treatment of hymn texts indicated that his thinking was moving steadily from an exclusively

Christian viewpoint to a perspective embracing the possibility of a moral spirituality that brings together people of all religions, or even people of no religion. He was becoming increasingly convinced that unity must arise from the whole of humanity, not just from within Christian denominations. There is a suggestion that the search for a god is ultimately the search for that which binds us together as human beings. Goodness is the peace and fulfilment that results from this joint exploration. The earliest text Fred wrote to articulate these ideas came about in the following way. Some friends who were not Christian believers, but aspired to a secular spirituality, wanted a hymn to celebrate their marriage. The hymn Fred wrote for them articulates the commitment of the marriage ceremony within the context of human love because 'on human loving peace on earth depends'. Throughout the text the focus is on the bride and groom supported by their friends at the beginning of their new life together. Some time after this hymn was first sung Fred received three other requests for wedding hymns. He obliged by sending three texts, including this most recent hymn for a 'not quite religious' wedding ceremony. He was amazed when he learned that this was the hymn chosen on each occasion, even though the original requests had come from two ministers and a church secretary!

As his thinking on the subject of multi-faith hymnody evolved, Fred began to rework some of his earlier texts. A vivid example of this is *Hands shaped like a cradle*, which started life as *Let hands speak out* and was one of the winning entries in the 1988 BBC *Songs of Praise* hymn-writing competition. The hymn points out the important part our hands play in the Christian Eucharist as they support a burning canᴅ. join in prayer and cradle the communion bread. In 1991, this hymn was sung at the first service of thanksgiving for the life and work of Bolton Hospice. The hymn was so popular that it was used at subsequent anniversaries of the hospice and even came to be referred to as 'the hospice hymn'. However, the hospice chaplaincy realised that more and more Muslim and Hindu relatives attended these services, a reflection of Bolton's increasing ethnic diversity. Clearly these members of the community might hesitate to join in with such words as:

> As at communion, shape your hands
> into a waiting cradle;
> the gift of Christ receive, revere,
> united round the table.

Even though the anniversary services were held in a church, they were not intended to be exclusively Christian in their message. The hospital chaplain, Revd Jim Hollyman, eventually contacted Fred to ask if he would be willing to write two new verses that might be more appropriate for a multi-faith occasion.

> Give thanks for strong – yet tender – hands,
> held out in trust and blessing.
> Where words fall short, let hands speak out,
> the heights of love expressing.

> Reach out in friendship, stay with faith
> in touch with those around you.
> Put peace into each other's hands:
> the Peace that sought and found you.

nd Anthea decided to settle in the Lake

into the bungalow, called *Marazan*, which

ted from her parents. Now that he was

...nty, Fred decided to reduce his preaching commitments and to concentrate on writing hymns and giving lectures on contemporary hymn writing. Fred's latest collection to date was published in 1999, planned to coincide with his seventieth birthday. *The Only Earth We Know* takes its name from the last line of the text *Imagination is a tree*. It is Fred's favourite among his own books, even though there is some repetition of material from other collections. Many of the texts have been updated since their original creation and the book has been widely acknowledged as a major contribution to contemporary hymnody.

At the beginning of the new millennium, Knut Nystedt and Fred were invited to collaborate on a large and prestigious project. This was for the world exhibition, *EXPO 2000*, which was to be held in Hanover, Germany. The conductor of a leading female choir, Professor Gudrun Schröfel, commissioned seven contemporary composers each to submit a choral work for the occasion. Fred wrote the libretto for Knut's contribution, *Magnificat for a New Millennium*, to be performed by mixed choir, four trombones and percussion. In his text Fred extends his concept of unity to draw attention to the tension between the fundamental elements of our planet – water, soil and air – and our abuse of these gifts. The work opens and closes with the call 'may confidence inspire our forward way' and urges us to be 'faithful in all the affairs of today'. Because the *Magnificat for a New Millennium* was the only one of the seven new pieces to deal exclusively with the dawning of a new era, it was decided that it should come at the very end of the two-evening presentation. It was an emotional end to the concert, all the more so as, coincidentally, it took place on Knut's 85th birthday.

Fred had now remained in contact with his close Canadian friend, Dr Ron Klusmeier, for thirty-three years. In 2001, Ron invited Fred to join him on an exciting tour of Canada called the *Wind of Change*. The tour was to start in Halifax, Nova Scotia, cross the whole of the North American continent and end on Vancouver Island – visiting a phenomenal forty-nine church communities in only fifty-two days! The idea of this tour was to present contemporary hymns in an innovative style using solo and choral vocalists. The accompaniments were frequently in a jazz style and there was also dancing. The texts, most of which were written by Fred, were given a short spoken introduction and Ron, who had written the tunes, conducted all the performances. Fred also seized the opportunity to speak about developments in contemporary hymn writing. Every venue was packed and there was an enthusiastic response on each occasion.

As a result of the success of the *Wind of Change* tour, Fred was invited to make a return trip to Canada in 2004 to give a series of lectures at the Vancouver School of Theology, University of British Columbia. The *G. Peter Kaye Lectures* are held annually at the Chalmers Institute for Continuing Education and Congregational Development. Since 1989 all the lecturers had been eminent theologians so Fred was intimidated – but rather pleased – to find himself among them! This feeling of satisfaction was deepened when he found out that the invitation had originally been issued to Dr Rowan Williams, the Archbishop of Canterbury, who, owing to the pressures of work, had been unable to accept. The organisers decided to approach their second choice – Dr Fred Kaan! Previous lectures in this series had been presented formally but Fred was keen that his talks should be illustrated with hymn-singing with live accompaniment. Although this was the first time such a request had been made, it was granted by the authorities and the subsequent outcome was greeted with delight by everyone present.

In January 2005, the 75-year-old Fred revisited Canada, again at the invitation of Ron Klusmeier, to take part in a new tour called *Song Circling all the Earth*. On this occasion they adopted a completely fresh approach to collecting and presenting material. The texts, by a number of contemporary hymn writers, dealt with each Sunday of the year starting with the Feast of the Epiphany. This meant that all the themes of the Christian year were treated in turn. Since the tour took place in January, the participants were able to look forward to the rest of the year by singing all the new hymns. Each performance lasted for over two hours. There was little speaking, but occasionally, the performance of a hymn would be interrupted by the original writer of the text stepping forward to read a verse or two in person. Once more the venues were full of enthusiastic congregations, all of whom revelled in the massive forces on display – a choir of over 150 singers, an orchestra and soloists – all directed by Ron Klusmeier from the piano.

Fred's interest in contemporary social themes was to find vivid expression in his hymns. He was commissioned to write hymns for a number of important gatherings. His concern with women's issues was demonstrated in 'God, you freed us to discover in our womanhood our role', which was commissioned by the Presbyterian Women of Wales for their Millennium Mission Rally. The hymn is hard-hitting in its direct reference to the continuing oppression of women – even in the twenty-first century:

> Teach us how to pray and practise
> 'NO' to what demeans, depraves;
> raise our voice for women, children
> sold and used, abused as slaves.

Fred was asked to contribute a hymn for a major international ecumenical conference on Christian Unity to be held at St Albans Cathedral, Hertfordshire in May 2003. The overall theme of the conference was *May they all be one – but how?* Fred took this theme as the title for his hymn. The hymn opens by raising the question of whether Christians should risk everything for the sake of uniting the Christian denominations:

> We meet, responsive to the Word of life,
> and take the questing path: the risk of faith;
> faith for the future, in our here-and-now,
> in search of 'May they all be one' – but how?

In 2005 Fred was asked to contribute a hymn for a Progressive Christianity Network conference held in London. Rather than offering an entirely new text, he decided to rework these two recent hymns, altering the language to reinforce the message. Both of these texts were accepted for the conference proceedings, and emphasise Fred's conviction that the whole of humanity needs to stand together for justice, for peace and for equality:

> We meet, exploring each new call of life
> and take the questing path: the risk of faith;
> faith for the future, in the here and now;
> hope bringing justice to our world – but how?

In my very first conversation with Fred Kaan, his argument for unity, not only among Christians but among all faiths, was compelling. 'If,' he said, 'we cannot agree to act together, what hope is there for us?'

> Let every human heart and door stand wide,
> and bread and wine to no one be denied.
> Let all the world united be! – but how?
> **Go out! Love people! In the here and now!**

# 11

## Back to Glenridding 2005

Unusually for the British climate, fine weather is coming in from the north-west. The beautiful sloping garden at *Marazan* is bathed with warm sunshine and Ullswater sparkles tantalisingly between the foliage. Fred Kaan and I have agreed to work outside so not a minute of the sun is wasted – after all, it could be gone as quickly as it arrived. Surrounded by papers, photographs and hymn books, it seems that Fred's entire hymn-writing career is spread about me. So, what next …? As we continue our discussions, Fred has this to say:

The hymn-writing part of my life has, over the years, brought me to recognise that the essential value of worship inside church lies in its bearing on what happens in people's day-to-day lives outside the church. After all, the greater part of a person's life is spent away from 'liturgical happenings'. I once put it this way in a hymn on *Worship and Practical Praise:*

> From Sunday to Monday
> the challenge remains:
> when worship is over,
> the service begins.

In fact, the most impressive church I ever preached in was in Kiribati in the Pacific. The building was simply a straw roof supported by wooden posts. All around us, there was the village, the world, the living-together of people – a whole society visible and audible from 'within' the church with the smell of cooking on wood-fires wafting into the congregation like a descant to our hymn-singing. A church without walls! I sometimes think if only the whole world were warm enough to dispense with walls altogether ...

Sadly, though, in assessing the validity of our faith, we are so often hedged in by declarations of exclusivity. Will human beings forever be judged by the religious labels they are forced to wear, or by the dogmas they are forced to take on board without question? At the 1975 Nairobi assembly of the World Council of Churches, delegates were deeply moved by a fascinating observation from Father Samuel Rayan, a Jesuit theologian, who pointed out:

> We need a multi-religious theology, a theology in the spirit of the greatest prayer of the church – the Our Father – which *all* people can say, and to which the church has *never* added: 'in the name of Jesus Christ'.

I must admit that it hit me between the eyes that the Lord's Prayer is never ended in the way almost all our prayers are rounded off!

I would not be so naive as to suppose that singing hymns in church is the only means of bringing the nations together. But if ever that day dawns when people of different races, cultures and faiths find their lives peacefully merging together, we in our country cannot fail, I believe, to reach out in spontaneous song and join with that greater, god-given harmony among nations.

# 12

## A Canadian Postscript:
## Life on the Road with Fred

### Contributed by Ron Klusmeier

Thousands of kilometres separate us, so we do not have frequent opportunities to be together face to face. Yet none of the distances of time or geography have diminished the truly kindred-spirit affection and connection I feel with Fred Kaan.

For almost my entire career in music and arts ministry, Fred has been mentor and friend. Long-time associations with hymn writers like Fred, Walter Farquharson, Brian Wren, Ruth Duck and Shirley Erena Murray have enriched and, indeed, shaped my personal theology. While it would be completely inappropriate to compare the influence any of these fine poets have had on me, it must be acknowledged that Fred Kaan holds a truly unique place in my life-journey.

Thanks largely to the initial vision and daring of the late Rev. Dr Stanley Osborne in the late 1960s and early 1970s, Fred Kaan has become a virtual household name in the Canadian church. The United Church of Canada, among other Canadian denominations, has embraced Fred's emphasis on social justice and his concept of the Christ being within and among us in our 'here and now'.

Together, Fred and I have criss-crossed this vast country by air, water and land, visiting everywhere from tiny rural communities to large urban centres. Together, we have presented concerts, led workshops and offered lectures in venues ranging from the town hall in Saltcoats, Saskatchewan to the Vancouver School of Theology. Together, we have 'grown' a friendship which has become deeper with each meeting – a friendship rooted in that sense of kindred spirit, in trust, and in laughter. Our mutual love of jokes and puns, of 'church silliness', and of the foolishness and folly of being ourselves has pushed us to near hysterical giggles in more private and public spaces than I could possibly recount. I have often wondered what some people must think as we enter a restaurant, hotel lobby, or church together with tears of laughter streaming down reddened cheeks. At the heart of that joyous laughter, for me, is the knowledge that each time we are together, I am aware of what a privilege it is to be in such intimate contact with this man of greatness. I do not use this terminology lightly. Fred's gifts to faith communities and, in fact, to all humankind will live on as long as there are people who are willing to struggle to be true to their faith and their calling, to be seekers of peace, and to colour outside the lines with vision and hope.

Stories of Kaan and Klusmeier are inevitably based from 'life on the road'. There is something very special about travelling together which becomes increasingly difficult to articulate. It is true that we have wonderful anecdotal stories which we both delight in sharing with friends on our respective sides of the Atlantic. But perhaps what has been the richest part of our journeys together has been the growth and depth of relationship we each acknowledge and treasure. I believe it is something similar to the way a marriage or life-partnership can mature, moving from those wonderful early times of infatuation to a point where words are often unnecessary. A blessed place in time where a knowing smile or a barely perceptible wink or nod from one to the other, and sometimes returned, speaks the volumes that words could (but no longer need to) convey.

The first Canadian tour we did together was in 1976. We had worked together a number of times prior to that, having been introduced personally to each other through the magic and ingenuity of the then editor of *The United Church Observer*, Al Forrest.

That 1976 tour saw us hopscotching across the country, flying every morning to a new destination, offering a workshop every afternoon, and a concert every evening. We would then head off to hotel rooms where we, of course, stayed up later than we should night after night. Morning was always amusing! It reached a point where we would see each other down a hallway or in a lobby and, despite being absolutely wrecked from the day and night before, we would break out into our morning giggles.

In 2001 we outdid ourselves. In the summer of 2000, I sent a fax to Fred suggesting it might be fun to 'do a little tour' in 2001 to celebrate the 25th anniversary of our first Canadian trip together. I didn't know how he would receive the idea since he and Anthea had, by this point, retired to the Lake District. Within hours, I had a very positive reply by return fax.

I started putting feelers out for possible venues. There was such excitement from churches right across Canada about the prospect of this tour that it just grew and grew. The 'little tour' became forty-nine concerts in fifty-two days from coast to coast! It started in Nova Scotia on the east coast (unfortunately, we weren't able to secure any venues in Newfoundland) and the tour was completed on the west coast's Vancouver Island.

We did the entire journey by land. Five of us (Fred, Anthea, Christina, me, and vocalist Sheelah Megill) travelled in our jeep pulling a trailer filled with equipment, luggage, books and CDs. Actually, the CDs and books were in 'kit form'. In the rush to get everything ready on time, the CDs had to be delivered to us unpackaged and the books had not been bound. Day after day for the first two weeks of the trip, we would set up an assembly line in whatever church we happened to be based for the day. All five of us would walk circles around a table, collating books and putting CD jewel cases together.

One would think that the reality of five adults driving together nearly every day in one small vehicle, being in a different community nearly every night, unloading and then reloading a trailer nearly every day, all would have taken a serious toll on both friendship and sanity. Remarkably, when we finished the tour, we each felt that we could begin it again 'in a heartbeat'.

*Ron Klusmeier*                                        *July 2005*

# Acknowledgements

The author and publishers gratefully acknowledge the assistance of the following in allowing reproduction of copyright material:

Revd Dr Fred Kaan for the quotation from the hymn text *The ship of goodwill* (pp.40–41) and the quotations from the foreword to the original 1967 edition of *Pilgrim Praise* (p.57); Pilgrim Church, Plymouth for the church mottoes and quotations from the church records (p.53); The South West Film and Television Archive and Revd Dr Fred Kaan for the quotations from the talks *Faith for Life* (p.63); Division of Christian Education of the National Council of the Churches of Christ in the USA for the scripture quotation from the Revised Standard Version of the Bible, © 1952 (2nd edition, 1971), all rights reserved (p.63); the United Reformed Church for the quotation from the report on the missionary strategy of the Congregational Church in England and Wales (p.65); World Council of Churches for the statement taken from their website (p.67) and the quotation from *Risk: New Hymns for a New Day* (Albert van den Heuvel), WCC Publications, 1966 (p.70); Hope Publishing Company for the quotation from Erik Routley's foreword to *Break Not the Circle* (p.75) and the quotation from *The Hymn*, October 1980 (p.84); Revd Phil Hoar, of Central Church, Swindon, for the quotations from *The Spokesman* (pp.97 and 98); University of Nebraska Press for the quotation from *Black Elk Speaks: Being the Life Story of a Holy Man of the Oglala Sioux* by John G. Neihardt, © 1932, 1959, 1972 by John G. Neihardt, © 1961 by the John G. Neihardt Trust, © 2000 by the University of Nebraska Press (p.101).

The photograph of Windsor Road Congregational Church, Barry is reproduced by kind permission of Revd Glanville Jones. The cover photographs were taken by the author. All other photographs courtesy of Fred Kaan.

Fred Kaan's collaborations with Knut Nystedt, *For a Small Planet*, *A Hymn of Human Rights*, *Magnificat for a New Millennium* and *One Mighty Flowering Tree* are available from Norsk Musikforlag A/S, PO Box 1499 – Vika, NO – 0116 Oslo, Norway. *Ave Christe* is available from Möseler Verlag, Hoffmann-v.-F.-Str. 8, 38304 Wolfenbüttel, Germany.